THE VIKINGS
AND THEIR ORIGINS

David M. Wilson

THE VIKINGS
AND THEIR ORIGINS

A & W Visual Library
New York

*Frontispiece: bronze brooch in the
Jellinge style, from Birka.*

*First published in the United States of America in 1980 by
A & W Publishers, Inc.
95 Madison Avenue
New York, New York 10016
By arrangement with Thames and Hudson, London, England*

*Library of Congress Catalog Card Number: 79-56390
ISBN: 0-89104-184-2*

Printed and bound in Great Britain

Contents

Preface

The Vikings were one of the most remarkable phenomena ever to burst on the European scene. Suddenly, apparently out of nowhere, waves of raiders appeared along the coastline of Western Europe. 'Never before', wrote Alcuin, the leading scholar of Europe, in 793, 'has such terror appeared in Britain as we have now suffered from a pagan race, nor was it thought that such an inroad from the sea could be made. Behold the church of St Cuthbert spattered with the blood of the priests of God, despoiled of all its ornaments; a place more venerable than all in Britain is given as a prey to pagan peoples.' The shock of this attack has burnt itself into the minds of European historians and scholars, many of whom to this day echo Alcuin's words and thoughts. But the Viking attacks do not reflect the situation in Scandinavia itself. For many Scandinavians who lived in the homeland throughout this traumatic period of their people's history, society and daily life did not change in any very marked fashion. The basic economy of Scandinavia was still, as it had been from the beginning of the millennium, pastoral or agrarian. It is my intention in this book to outline the Viking adventure against the background of the Scandinavians in their homeland. The development seen in Scandinavian society from the birth of Christ to the end of the Viking Age, about 1100, is a continuous one – the gradual emergence of a group of pagan tribes into a Christian community accepted by its peers in Western Europe. The adventures of the Vikings in Russia, Ireland, England, America and Byzantium – important though they may be – are incidental to this process. Christianity and its concomitant, literacy, was the catalyst which finally accomplished the change.

A book of this length, expanded from a single chapter in a large volume that dealt with the whole of the Western world of the first millennium AD, cannot be more than a sketch of a people living in a vast tract of country at a time of great political, economic and religious change over a period of about a thousand years. It is intended to introduce the general reader to a most fascinating period in the history of Scandinavia – a period represented in the archaeological record by outstanding and beautiful finds and revealed to our eye in some cases by the most advanced archaeological techniques.

In writing this book I have relied to a great extent on many friends in the Scandinavian countries who have discussed the various problems of the period with me and allowed me to study material and collections in their care. Particularly I value many years of friendship with my teacher, the late Holger Arbman, professor of prehistoric and medieval archaeology in the University of Lund, who was perhaps the greatest Viking archaeologist of his generation. To his memory I dedicate this small offering.

D.M.W.

1 The unveiling of Scandinavia

Scandinavia is a vast area: a straight line drawn from southern Jutland to the northernmost point of Norway would measure some twelve hundred miles in length, a distance greater than that between southern Jutland and Rome. The southernmost part of Scandinavia lies on the same latitude as Newcastle; North Cape in Norway lies 235 miles north of the Arctic Circle. The area is united nowadays by its people, its blood-ties and its geographical situation as the north-western corner of Europe. Physically it is united only by the sea; the lush pastures of Jutland, the rich farm lands of Skåne and South Norway, bear little relationship to the high fells of Norway or the forests of Swedish Småland. The variation in climate is enormous and the natural economy varies accordingly.

The classical sources

This vast area was hardly known to the Roman world at the beginning of our era. Pytheas, three hundred years earlier, had described – albeit at second hand – what must be Norway to the sceptical scientists of the Mediterranean. He labelled it *Thule*, where, 'for lack of the crops and cattle of more genial lands, its inhabitants subsist on wild berries and "millet" which they thresh in covered barns because of the continual rains. From the plentiful honey of their bees they prepare mead as a drink.' Few of his contemporaries and successors believed Pytheas, but gradually more information began to filter through to the classical world and so to posterity. The Romans came into direct contact with the Scandinavians in AD 5, when a Roman fleet made a reconnaissance to the Skaw, the northernmost tip of Jutland. Pliny the Elder, Tacitus and Ptolemy mention several tribes in this area, including the *Suiones*, who must almost certainly be the Swedes (*Svíar*) of Uppland who were to become the richest tribe in Scandinavia and whose territory was to be the kernel of the modern Swedish kingdom. Tacitus tells us that:

> The shape of their ships differs from the normal in having a prow at both ends, they do not rig sails or fasten their oars in banks at the side. . . . Wealth, too, is held in high honour and that is why they obey one rule, with no restrictions on his [the ruler's] authority and with no mere casual claim to obedience. Arms are not, as in the rest of Germany, allowed to all and sundry, but are kept under guard, and the guard is a slave.

At a later date Ptolemy, who wrote in Egypt about AD 150, named a number of tribes including the *Goutoi* (who are almost certainly the *Gautar* – the *Geatas* of the great Anglo-Saxon epic *Beowulf*) and the *Chaideinoi* (who are probably to be identified with the Norwegian *Heidnir*).

For nearly three hundred years the Scandinavians pass out of literature and, since they were themselves to all intents illiterate, our knowledge of them must rest on the vast corpus of archaeological remains meticulously excavated by Scandinavian scholars in the last 150 years. It is remarkable that the Romans never tried to conquer the Scandinavian tribes, but it seems likely that after the crushing defeat of Varus at the hands of the *Teutones* in AD 9 the Romans decided not to attempt the conquest of a distant land, the tribes of which were apparently permanently locked in internecine war: political and military considerations apparently outweighed the obvious economic potential of the North. Trade with the North was, however, encouraged and, until the frontiers of the Roman Empire exploded in the third century, trade flowed to the mutual advantage of both Scandinavia and Rome.

The Roman Iron Age   Although the archaeological evidence is the main source of knowledge of the first four hundred years of our era in Scandinavia, the dominating influence of a literate empire has caused the period to be labelled 'the Roman Iron Age'. The label is justified if only because exotic goods originating in the Roman Empire form the most obtrusive element in the rich archaeology of southern Scandinavia. Much of this material came to Scandinavia by means of trade – an activity which was not new to the Scandinavians, who for many years had had a lively commercial contact with southern Europe.

Most of the imported objects found in Scandinavia come from the grave-finds and it is a fortunate coincidence that at this period, in the richer parts of Scandinavia at least, the rite of inhumation gradually replaced the hitherto prevailing rite of cremation. The reason for this basic change is not known, but it may have been due in part to contact with the religion of the inhabitants of Silesia and Central Europe. The new rite enables archaeologists to gain a more complete view of the material culture and economy of the Scandinavian people through studying the objects which accompanied the dead to the grave. Inhumation, however, was not universal; cremation and inhumation burials occasionally occur alongside each other, while cremation was still particularly favoured in Norway, where cemeteries of upwards of a thousand graves have been recorded. The Roman objects found in the inhumation graves are mainly luxury goods – bronze (and even silver) vessels, glass bowls, brooches, moulded red Samian ware (*terra sigillata*) and the occasional bronze figure of a Roman god.

Many of the objects reached Scandinavia by trade routes which were apparently controlled by the *Marcomanni*, a tribe – settled at this period in Bohemia – who acted as middlemen between the Celts, Scandinavians and Romans. Merchants, leaving the security of the Roman Empire, crossed the Danube between Vienna and Linz, travelled through their territory to the Elbe and the Oder and so to the Baltic and Scandinavia. A secondary trade route led from the mouth of the Rhine, along the Frisian coast to the western seaboard of Scandinavia, and is demonstrated archaeologically by the presence in these areas of Roman silver coins (*denarii*) – a sure clue to the passage of Roman trade. This western route, and an eastern one along the Vistula, were to become much more important later in the Roman period.

The Roman imports found in Scandinavia are, of course, merely fossils of a considerable trade; other goods of a more perishable nature also came from the South but have left no record in the archaeological material. Among these objects of trade must have been silks and other textiles, spices and, almost certainly, wine. That the inhabitants of these cold northern countries had a considerable interest in alcohol is attested by the large number of drinking-vessels, including many drinking-horn mounts, found in the graves. Richer members of the community would presumably have been only too pleased to supplement their native drinks of mead and beer with imported Mediterranean wines.

8

In return for these luxuries the Scandinavians probably exported goods of the type for which there is literary evidence at a later period – furs, skins, ropes made of sealskin, dairy produce and even cattle. Slaves also were probably one of the most important exports of Scandinavia. Another popular export in both prehistoric and historic times was Baltic amber, a substance which fetched high prices in the Mediterranean. The importance of the amber trade has, however, almost certainly been over-emphasized by archaeologists who have been fascinated by the amount of amber found in southern Europe, for some of it is certainly not of Baltic origin.

The luxury trade, naturally, makes the greatest impact on the modern eye. Although the perishable goods have disappeared, there are, in the Scandinavian graves, such extraordinary testimonies to the far-flung trading connections of the period as the Danish grave-find of Hoby, on the island of Lolland. Chief among the objects buried in this grave are two silver beakers of remarkable quality made by a Greek craftsman – Cheirisophos – who must have been active in Rome in the first century AD. The grave also contained a skillet made in Capua and two bronze vessels of exceptionally high quality, as well as a salver, a dish and a bucket. The silver cups bear Homeric scenes – Priam and Achilles, Odysseus and Philoctectus – a jug is decorated with a vine-scroll, while Venus appears with a group of cupids on the bronze dish.

Luxuries from the south

These objects are among the finest Roman products found in Scandinavia; but others, only slightly less impressive, have come from graves and bogs throughout Denmark, in south and central Sweden – particularly in the rich areas of Uppland and Gotland – and to a lesser extent in Norway. At Fycklinge, in Västmanland in central Sweden, for example, was found a most impressive bronze vessel some 50 cm high. It is inlaid with silver and copper and is inscribed 'to Apollo Grannus this gift is offered by the benefactor of the temple Ammillus Constans.' Another bronze vessel, plundered from a temple (probably in Gaul), was found in Vang in Hedemark, Norway; it bears the inscription, 'Aprus and Livertinus gave this vessel to the temple.' Two splendid glass vessels from Himmlingøje, Sjælland, one of which is decorated with a series of coloured animals including a splendid blue leopard, witness to the Scandinavian taste for Roman luxury articles – whether as the products of trade, as loot or as diplomatic gifts.

But the Himmlingøje grave is one of the later graves of the Roman Iron Age and it is clear that the import trade changed towards the end of the second century, presumably when the Marcomannic kingdom was destroyed after the attack on the Danubian frontier of the Roman Empire in 165 and after the settlement of the frontier by the Goths (who began to control the trade of Central Europe in the course of the third century). From this time forward the quality of the goods imported from the Roman world into Scandinavia declined considerably as the axis of direct trade shifted westwards. Later Roman objects found in Scandinavia were mostly made in the province of Gaul. The mercantile activity which imported material of this character must have been backed by fairly sophisticated trading stations, which may have been of a semi-permanent nature. It has been suggested, for example, that in the fourth century there were minor market-places which dealt in Roman goods in southern Vestfold (in South Norway) which drew on both the Baltic and the North Sea for their goods.

9

During the whole of the Roman Iron Age there was considerable contact between Scandinavia and the eastern Mediterranean by way of the rivers of Eastern Europe, particularly the Vistula. The routes themselves are not very easy to trace, but the mapping of antiquities does occasionally indicate the areas in the Baltic where the objects eventually emerged. Typical evidence of such contacts are the seven thousand *denarii*, spanning the whole of the Roman period, which have been found in Sweden – five thousand of them on the island of Gotland. They probably came thither by way of the Russian and Polish rivers, along which are found a large number of similar hoards. Most of these coins must have come through contact with the Goths – a tribe which may originally have been Scandinavian and which was certainly at one time settled on the South Baltic coast. Its members established themselves on the shores of the Black Sea in the early third century and spread thence into Central Europe. Such coin hoards do not reflect a monetary economy, rather they must be seen as bullion – a symbol and fact of wealth.

The remarkable treasure from Havor, Hablingbo, Gotland, must also be considered as a reflection of wealth. It was discovered in 1961 within the banks of a fortified encampment and consists of a shouldered bronze pail, 33 cm high, a matching ladle and strainer (the latter stamped with the maker's name – CANNISMASVIT), three other ladles, two bronze bells and – most remarkable of all – a gold neck-ring more than 24 cm in diameter, beautifully decorated with filigree. The handle of the pail is supported by cast brackets in the form of human masks. It is of Campanian origin, while the neck-ring must have had its origin in South Russia. It has been suggested that the ring was not intended to be worn by a human, but rather that it adorned an idol, and the excavator of the find has tentatively suggested that the hoard may represent the treasure of a temple. Such a hypothesis is interesting but coincidental to the indications it gives of the trading connections of the Swedes and the wealth of the Scandinavians as revealed by this treasure. Eastern imports have also been encountered in Norway: certain objects in a rich grave of the fourth century from Sætrang, not far from Oslo, have been shown to have come from south-eastern Europe, by way of the Baltic.

The runes   An element in Scandinavian culture which may have come to Scandinavia by the same route as the gold collar from Havor is literacy, which is first indicated in Scandinavia by the runes, which appear towards the end of the second or at the beginning of the third century of our era. They are first found, for example, on weapons from Moos in Gotland and Stabu, some seventy-five miles north of Oslo, where they presumably spell out the name given to the weapon by its first owner – a practice documented in early Germanic literature. The earliest Scandinavian runic alphabet occurs on a stone of the late fourth or early fifth century from a cist grave at Kylver in Gotland. The first six letters of the inscription give the name – *fuþark* – to the Scandinavian runic alphabet. The main inscription reads *fuþarkgwhnijpèRstbemlngdo*; this is followed by an uninterpretable sign which looks like a fir-tree and, a little above and to the right, the five letters *sueus* (apparently a meaningless word). It can be seen from the idealized runic alphabet shown in pl. 88 that the runic letters were made up in almost every case of straight strokes, ideally suited for carving across the grain of wood or on stone. From the Roman Iron Age onwards this form of writing appears in an unbroken sequence, mostly occurring on objects of stone and wood, right through to the nineteenth century. Wood was the natural medium of this strange alphabet, as is well demonstrated by the vast amount of medieval material found during the excavations in the medieval town of Bergen in Norway, where texts vary from 'lavatory-wall' inscriptions to trading documents and private letters. It is unfortunate that most of the inscriptions that are to be dated within the period covered by this book are on sepulchral or memorial monuments, or on weapons – the wooden evidence has almost completely disappeared.

Runes are widely considered to be endowed with magical significance. That there undoubtedly was a magical or religious element in the character of the runes is illustrated by the fact that the Kylver inscription occurs on a stone buried in a grave as well as by a passage from the early Scandinavian poem *Hávamál*:

> I know that I hung on the windswept tree for nine whole nights pierced by the spear, given to Odin, myself given to myself on that tree whose roots no man knows. They refreshed me neither with bread nor with drink from the horn. I peered down, I learnt runes, howling I learnt them, and then fell back.

There seems, however, no reason to suppose that runes were necessarily magical or religious in origin; it would seem probable that they were primarily and originally used for purposes of normal communication and that they were adapted for religious and magical purposes in an incidental fashion.

The origin of the runes themselves is obscure. They were certainly not a Scandinavian invention and tentative theories would now derive them from the Greek, Roman or North Italic-Celtic alphabets, perhaps along the eastern or (less likely) perhaps along the western routes. However we interpret the runes and with whatever origins we endow them, they provide the first evidences of literacy in Scandinavia. From the time of their first appearance the historical record becomes less dark, although it is not until the Viking Age that they add in any marked degree to our knowledge of the Scandinavian people.

From the grave-goods of the Scandinavians in the Roman Iron Age we can see that they were considerably influenced by fashions current in the Roman provinces and in the lands of the Germanic tribes who were clients of the Romans or lived on the borders of the Empire. The shapes and designs of the arm-rings, brooches and gold pendants worn by the men and women, and the forms of some of the pottery which was used for both cooking and storage, were based to some extent on Roman models. Roman ornamental motifs were incorporated into their own art. Occasionally they even attempted to reproduce Roman representational art in their own idiom: provincial Roman statues were copied, drained of naturalism and strengthened by abstract individuality. Roman designs formed the basis for the lively art of the Migration Period which is discussed below.

Their weapons, their clothes and many other aspects of their material culture, however, had nothing to do with the Roman world. The drinking-horns, which have already been mentioned, were not the sort of thing one would expect to see on any self-respecting Roman's table. The weapons – shield, spear and sword – were quite unlike those carried by the regular Roman armies, although the sword, a long-bladed weapon of hard steel, carried in a scabbard which was slung from the belt, was similar in form to that used by the Germanic auxiliaries of the Roman army. The

Weapons and dress

11

Decorated leather belt-end from the bog-find at Vimose. The ornament is derived from a Roman motif. Such belts were decorated with circular bronze mounts, which were fastened by means of a lug passing through a slit in the leather.

shield was made of thin wooden board with a central iron boss to protect the hand: it was light and was normally circular, although rectangular shields are also known. The spear, with a leaf-shaped blade, and the bow and arrow completed the warrior's armament.

We know little of the dress of the Scandinavians in this period, although a series of finds from the bogs of South Jutland and North Germany give some indication of fashion. The men wore trousers, one pair of which has attached foot-pieces. The trousers were held in place by leather belts, some of which may have been decorated. The upper part of the body was covered by a jerkin and most men also wore a cloak. Women's clothes of this period have not survived to any great extent; what few clues we have would suggest that they wore a long trailing gown, perhaps made of a single rectangle of cloth fastened at the shoulders by a pair of brooches. To these basic garments would be added hats, shoes and cloaks. Hair was probably elaborately dressed and the men were usually clean-shaven. Most of the surviving dress is of wool, but one must presume that skins and furs were used and traces of linen are also found. The wool appears to have been woven on an upright loom which had a horizontal beam from which the warps were hung and weighted by stones or baked clay rings. The hems of some garments were probably braided in complicated patterns by tablet-weaving.

Although there was a considerable amount of Scandinavian capital tied up in trade, the basic economy of the country was essentially agricultural. The farmer tilled his land with an ard – a crooked stick with a point – which was dragged through the ground by an ox or by another human being. The heavier plough, with wheel and mould-board, is not attested in Scandinavia (according to recent radiocarbon dating) until well after the end of the first millennium of our era. Traces of furrows made by an ard were discovered during excavations at Nørre Fjand in Jutland – appearing as dark stripes running criss-cross over the surface of the fields parallel with the boundaries. Terraced fields divided by banks were also observed; the fields varied in size between about a quarter and three-quarters of an acre. Evidence concerning the crops grown at this period is slight; but from Bornholm we have some indication that barley and oats were grown at different periods of the Roman Iron Age. Harvesting implements of iron are frequently found and the harvested grain was ground on the common saddle-quern which had still not been replaced by the rotary quern. The grain was made into porridge or bread, which was baked either on open fires or in ovens – like the semicircular example found at Dalshøj on the Danish island of Bornholm. Nothing is perhaps so evocative of the everday life of the ordinary people as a small bread roll from Vikbolandet in Östergötland, Sweden. Sheep, cattle and goats provided meat, dairy produce and clothing for the people, but only the strongest beasts were kept throughout the winter: there would be a large slaughter of all sub-standard animals in the late autumn and their meat, together with fish from the sea, lakes and rivers, would be dried, smoked or salted away against the hard winter months.

Settlements and houses

The best evidence for houses of the Roman Iron Age comes from excavations in Denmark. Norway and Sweden have also produced a few settlement sites but the vast area of these countries makes it impossible to generalize concerning them. In fact, so rarely have settlements of this period been found in Sweden, north of what

12

was for much of its history a Danish province (Skåne), that it is practically impossible to say anything about the form houses took in that country. It is even impossible to say with any certainty whether the common form of settlement in Sweden was the farm or the village, and yet many burial-places, cemeteries and grave-fields are known for which a settlement site has yet to be discovered. Apart from the few houses which have been excavated in Rogaland, evidence for Norwegian settlement sites is sparse.

In Denmark a fair number of farms and villages have been excavated and the evidence suggests that villages were already in existence there at the beginning of our era. Basically the house types follow the form of the earlier houses of the pre-Roman Iron Age and certain generalizations can be made about them. They are rectangular in plan and, save in Fyn where the ridge of the roof was carried on a row of central upright posts, normally had a roof carried on a double row of posts which were presumably tied together in pairs by a cross-beam. The house was either a single chamber or was divided into two by a transverse screen; at one end were the living quarters, a single room with a hearth, and at the other end was a byre. At Ginderup, in North Jutland, the village had been destroyed by fire; in the fire the roof of one of the houses had fallen and the charred remains revealed that it had been supported on rafters between 4 cm and 8 cm thick, the rafters themselves having been covered by straw and two layers of turf. The house measured 14·75 × 4 m. The east end consisted of a byre with an earth floor, while the living quarters with a clay floor were at the west end. There was a stone-paved entrance in the middle of one of the long sides and underneath it the skeleton of a dog was found – an offering to the gods for the protection of the house. Another house at the same site, which had also been burnt down, had been abandoned with some animals still in the byre–four sheep, a pig and a cow. The buildings at Ginderup varied in detail and, as we examine the different house on Danish settlement sites of the Roman Iron Age in Jutland, we can see many such variations: at Nørre Fjand the walls were of wattle and daub, or in one case of upright posts, while at Ginderup there is some evidence of turf walls panelled with wood. The remains of a door at Nørre Fjand, 1·25 m high, perhaps give some indication of the height of the walls of the building.

All the indoor activities of human life took place in one long, hall-like chamber, usually with a central fire-place. Cooking, sleeping, spinning and quarrelling must have given to these smoky rooms an almost 'gothick' gloom.

The sea was an important element in the life of the Scandinavian peasant; from the sea he drew food, by way of the sea came traders and invaders. We are fortunate in having a fair amount of evidence concerning the ships of the first millennium. All the surviving ships of the pre-Viking era in Scandinavia were propelled by oars and there is no archaeological evidence that sail was used in Scandinavian waters before the Vikings emerged to trouble the world in the late eighth century. The Nydam vessels were found in the last century in a bog in South Jutland and are now in the Schleswig-Holstein Provincial Museum in Schleswig. The largest Nydam vessel is 23·7 m long and was made of oak. Its ribs are formed of natural-grown crooks, to which the planks were tied – clinker fashion – through cleats fashioned out of the solid wood. There is, practically speaking, no keel – merely a thickened plank – and there is no seating for a mast (the smaller boat from Nydam which was built of pine

The sea

13

has a slightly more elaborate keel). The rowlocks consist of thorn-shaped pieces of wood lashed to the gunwales and the longish sweeps survive. Boats such as this were large enough to cross the North Sea – after all many an eighteenth-century privateer was no larger – and it may have been in boats like these that the Anglo-Saxons came to England from this very area. Indeed a similar boat, some 26 m in length, was found at Sutton Hoo in Suffolk, in the grave-like cenotaph of an Anglo-Saxon king who was buried at some date between 625 and 635.

The Kvalsund find from Norway also consists of two ships found in a bog. The largest was 18 m in length, clinker-built of eight strakes fastened to natural-grown ribs. It has a modest keel and a steering oar on the starboard side. This boat is usually – but tentatively – dated to the seventh century, long after the Roman Iron Age but before the great Viking ships were developed. It has been suggested that the Kvalsund boat may have been rigged for sailing; this is not the place to discuss the possibility of the existence of sailing-ships in Scandinavian waters in the pre-Viking Age, but it should be remembered that Tacitus and other classical authors write convincingly of just such vessels in the southern North Sea at the very beginning of our era – perhaps the archaeological record gives a false picture, based purely on coincidence and accident.

Offerings and the gods

Both the Kvalsund and Nydam boats were recovered from bogs. The practice of ritual deposition of all sorts of objects is known from many sites in Scandinavia. It is estimated that from the Danish finds from Vimose, Ejsbøl, Kragehul, Nydam, Thorsbjerg and Illerup between fifteen thousand and twenty thousand objects have been recovered. In Norway and Sweden such deposits are less frequently encountered and are less rich, but such finds as those from Kvalsund in Norway and from Käringsjön and Skedemosse in Sweden indicate that the practice was widespread. Besides boats, weapons, treasures of gold and silver, clothing, idols, coins, animals and even human beings were placed in these bogs as a sacrifice to the gods. Not only the animals but the weapons themselves were sometimes 'killed' before being placed in the bog: gold and silver objects were bent or rolled up, swords were bent, spears were broken and shields were pierced before being thrown into the bog. Such finds may reflect Julius Caesar's description of the practice of certain German tribes:

> They dedicate to Mars [*i.e.* Odin], when they have determined on a decisive battle, such spoil as they may take. When they have conquered, they sacrifice such living things as they have captured and all the other effects they collect into one place. In many states you may see piles of these things heaped up on consecrated spots; nor does it often happen that anyone, disregarding the sanctity of the practice, has dared either to hide captured objects in his house, or take away those things set aside; and the severest punishment, with torture, has been ordained for such a deed.

The practice described by Caesar differs in some respects from that encountered in the Scandinavian bog finds, but the fundamental idea may be the same. Although there is a warlike character about many of the finds, they were not assembled and sacrificed at one time but over hundreds of years. At Skedemosse on the Swedish island of Öland, for example, the finds span the period from the third to the sixth

14

century, apart from certain offerings of animals, which have been dated by the radiocarbon method to the period about the birth of Christ. At Skedemosse – as at Ejsbøl – the finds were flung into a lake after the objects had been violently mutilated and often burnt. Human bones of some fifty individuals were also found; they may represent prisoners of war or people chosen specially for sacrifice. Strangely there were no finds of female equipment at Skedemosse – unlike at Thorsbjerg, for example.

It must be emphasized that the offerings have different characteristics at different periods. At Skedemosse we have seen how the earliest finds are largely seasonal offerings of slaughtered animals – representing, presumably, some aspect of prayer for fertility. In the third century the deposition becomes more warlike in character. The fertility aspect of such offerings is demonstrated at Käringsjön in southern Sweden, where wooden farming implements and traces of animal fat, even a bundle of flax, as well as animal bones, were discovered. Such finds can only be seen as reflections of the religion and superstitions of the Scandinavian people; they must be interpreted as thank-offerings, dedicatory offerings, or placatory gifts.

Until their conversion to Christianity – an object not achieved until the tenth and eleventh centuries – the Scandinavians worshipped a pantheon of gods who have an origin in the common Indo-European tradition. The gods were equated by classical authors with their Roman counterparts – Thor, for example, is similar in many of his aspects to Jupiter. The chief evidence concerning the nature of northern religion comes from medieval Christian sources which were, of course, hostile to such strange gods, but an occasional reference can also be culled from classical texts and poetic sources of the Viking Age. The chief gods were Odin, Thor, Njord and Frey. Odin was the god of poetry, the master of magic; he had great power and knowledge, he could hear the grass grow. He was also the god of war and all his followers who fell in battle joined him in Valhalla where they lived a fully heroic life of feasting and fighting. A more popular god – although not so powerful as Odin – was Thor, whose name is associated with thunder: he was immensely strong (his mother was Jörd, which is to be translated as 'Earth'). His symbol – the hammer Mjollnir – was very popular as an amulet in Scandinavia and presumably symbolizes his immense physical strength as well as his function as protector of the gods and men. The symbol may well have been used in the consecration of a bride and in association with the burial of the dead. Thor was red-haired, a mighty eater and toper, and rather unsophisticated. Njord was the god of wealth and, like his son Freyr, was associated with fertility. There were other deities, among them Baldr, Tyr, Bragi, and a number of goddesses including Odin's wife Frigg, and Freyja, the goddess of love. The gods lived in Asgard where each had his own hall; here also was Yggdrasil, the sacred tree, beneath which lived the three norns – representing past, present and future – who spin out man's destiny.

Norse mythology is permeated by the principle of evil and leads logically to the destruction of the world (Ragnarök) in which it and the gods are consumed by fire and water in the middle of a battle which has raged between the gods and the forces of evil, led by Loki, the instigator of all men's misfortunes. After Ragnarök a new world arises to which the gods return and where happiness, wisdom and fertility come into their own; goodness finally fills everything.

This was not a centrally organized religion; although there were cult places, temples and altars (some of which were more important than others), there was no

The story of Sigurd is shown, in part, on a fragment of a memorial slab from Kirk Andreas, Isle of Man. Interlaced animals fill the shaft of a cross. To the left, at the bottom, Sigurd slays the dragon; at the top he is shown roasting the heart of the dragon over a fire, the flames of which are represented by three triangles.

strict religious discipline. The priests were not set apart, and in isolated regions the temples were probably served by the rich landowners. There was no recognized doctrine, no uniform method of worship; a man chose his own god and went his own way, calling on different gods in different circumstances. In this lack of organization lay the relatively quick collapse of the pagan religion in the face of the Christian Church. It was not difficult to worship the Christian god at the same time; we are told, for example, that a Viking, Helgi the Lean, 'believed in Christ and yet made vows to Thor for sea-voyages or in tight corners, and for everything which struck him as of real importance.' But once Christ was admitted to the pagan pantheon it would not be long before the ancient gods fell to a doctrinally disciplined religious system.

It is against this background – a background of warlike gods and gods of fertility – that we must see the Scandinavian votive deposits, and, although they lose their war-like aspect in the sixth century, it is possible to trace in the 'killed' objects found in the graves of the Vikings something of the same religious tradition. The votive deposits and the graves, which contain articles of everyday use intended to accompany the dead person to the future life, provide our chief archaeological evidence for the religion of the North. Archaeological evidence for temples and cult sites has recently been weighed in the balance and found wanting and increased knowledge of these matters awaits further excavation and more critical investigation. Figures of gods are occasionally found. Thor and Freyr can be identified and Thor's hammer is frequently recognized in the Viking Period; it is even possible that figures incised on the memorial stones of Gotland represent Baldr, Odin and the other gods while certain divine heroes, such as Gunnar and Sigurd, appear frequently in Viking Age carving. These latter representations often occur in Christian contexts, obviously invested with a Christian meaning, and so, although the pagan religion disappeared, the Church retained some of the stories and converted them to its own use.

16

Hilt and scabbard mouth of a sixth-century sword from grave V at Snartemo, Hägebostad, Vest Agder, Norway. The grip is covered with gold plate; the other mounts are silver-gilt, all decorated in Style I. (1)

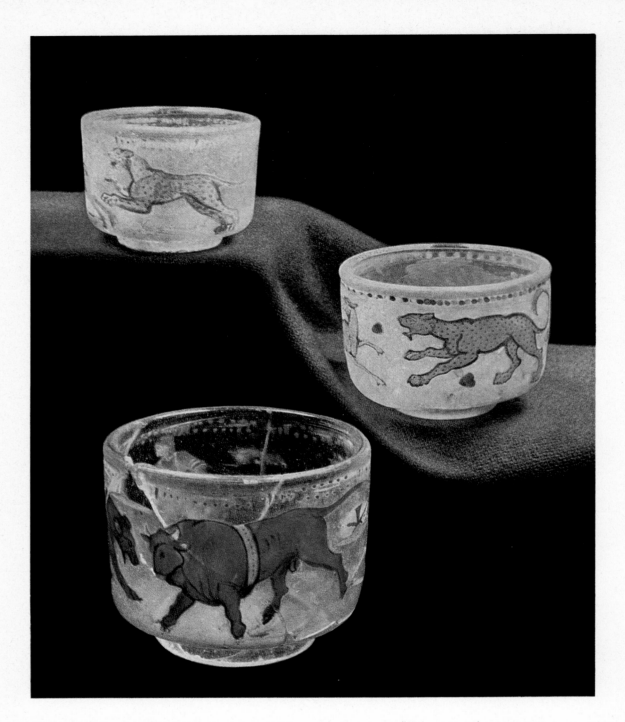

Imports from the Roman world

An obvious luxury, Roman imports in the north reveal but one facet of a considerable trade over much of Europe. The perishable goods that moved in and out of Scandinavia have left no trace in the archaeological record, but glass and bronze vessels must have been traded in some quantity northwards. These three imported glass vessels (above) are from graves in Denmark. All are decorated with animal friezes. The largest, bearing the figure of a bull, is dated about AD 200; the other pair dates from the end of the third century. (2)

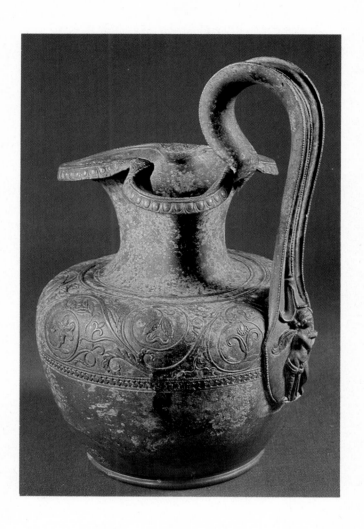

Elegant vine-scroll decorates an imported bronze jug (above) from the grave at Hoby, Denmark, which also contained the objects illustrated in pl. 31. At the base of the handle is a figure of Cupid. A Roman object of the finest Augustan quality, it is the only one of its type found in Denmark.

The inscription on the right is from a large bronze vessel (see pl. 28) found in a grave at Fycklinge, Björksta, Västmanland, Sweden. Originally from a Roman temple, it reads: APPOLINI GRANNO DONVM AMMILIVS CONSTANS PRAEF TEMPLI IPSIVS VSLLM (see p. 9). (3, 4)

Chieftains' armour

Rich Swedish chiefs from the province of Uppland were buried in boats with full panoply of war. These two helmets are among the most striking remains from their graves. Below: from grave XIV at Vendel. The iron cap is covered with impressed bronze panels which portray a procession of warriors (around the rim) and a scene of fighting men (above the eye-brows). The neck-guard and face mask are also made of iron, while the nose-guard is of bronze. Right: from grave I at Vendel. Constructed like the other helmet, its applied plates portray scenes of an armed rider and of a bear; a face appears at the bridge of the nose. (5, 6)

Sea-power

Command of the sea was the clue to the success of the Scandinavians in the Viking Age. The surviving ships are the most impressive monuments of this period. Those depicted here come from royal graves in southern Norway. General duty craft, they were capable of being used in the open sea and in shallow water (they would draw a mere 90 cm of water). The rising stem of the Oseberg ship (left) is carved with animal ornament of the early ninth century. The undecorated Gokstad ship (right) is dated to the late ninth century on the basis of finds associated with it. Top above: a detail of the tiller of the Gokstad ship shows surviving traces of paint; underneath is a detail of a prow ornament from Midtvåge, Onarheim, Tysnes, Norway. (7–10)

Icon or image?

Enigmatic, artistically superb, these three images, all from Oseberg, tease the imagination. Nowhere is the competence of the Scandinavian craftsmen better expressed than in woodcarving. The lion's head of the animal-headed post (left) is covered with animal ornament in the same style as that on the prow of the ship (pl. 52) and is possibly carved by the same craftsman. The restraint shown by the artist in leaving the neck undecorated is rarely encountered in Viking art. The grim faces of the two men (above and left) come from the cradle of the wagon (pl. 17), which may well have been the funerary cart. These strange masks could express thoughts connected with the after-life: we shall never know their meaning and it is futile to try and interpret them. (11–13)

A Queen's burial

The rich furnishings of a ninth-century royal household are represented here by objects from the great Oseberg ship-burial. Below: a *rangle*, an effective rattle used as a part of a sledge or wagon harness. Harness mounts complete the picture. (14)

Laced boots and shoes are mostly found on Viking town sites, less commonly in graves. These boots are among the best preserved of the period. (15)

Household utensils included a lamp, a long-handled flat griddle and a cauldron, the two latter for use over an open fire in the middle of the living room. Unusually, the cauldron hangs in a tripod, more normally it would have been suspended from a convenient beam. (16)

The impressive wagon from the Oseberg grave (top) has a detachable body and most certainly was made for ceremonial purposes; it may even have been specially built for the funeral itself. A number of cart bodies have been recognized recently in graves of the Viking Age: all, like this one, are from female graves. The chest (below) is one of a number found at Oseberg. Cupboards were unknown at this period and this would have been the main type of storage. (17, 18)

Riches from far

Wealth was expressed most palpably in gold and silver coins and jewellery. Until the Scandinavians settled overseas they did not (save in southern Denmark) strike coins themselves. As merchants, they were familiar with the idea of a monetary economy, and in foreign markets – and even at home – would presumably have used coins as currency. But gold and silver had value as bullion and its origin was immaterial. Islamic, Byzantine, Anglo-Saxon, Frankish and German coins bear witness to the widespread commerce of the Scandinavians. Gold was rare, and the ninth-century hoard from Hon in Norway (opposite), which is almost completely made up of gold objects, is unusual. It includes a Frankish trefoil brooch, an Anglo-Saxon finger-ring, a Byzantine armlet and a number of Scandinavian objects, including the great neck-rings.

More common are silver hoards like that from Birka, Sweden (above left), dated about 975, which comprises coins (mostly from the Arab caliphates) and arm-rings and brooches of local manufacture. The rough-cut lengths of silver to the left show that the metal was regarded as bullion. Similar hoards occur in the colonies. The hoard from Skaill, Orkney (which was deposited about 950), part of which is shown here (left), included coins from the caliphates and southern England. (19, 20, 21)

Busy ornament

Intricate creatures in silver wire (left) cover an inlaid axe. The axe was the weapon of the Vikings *par excellence*: this one, from Mammen, Jutland, Denmark, demonstrates the symbolic importance sometimes attached to such weapons. The great winged beast represented here has given its name to the Mammen style. Another beast is shown on the weather-vane above, an object of a type represented on graffiti of ships found at various Viking sites. This early eleventh-century example comes from Heggen in Norway. The strap mount of gilt-bronze (below) is from Broa, on the Swedish island of Gotland. With Style III animal ornament, it dates from the early ninth century and demonstrates the great skill of the jeweller of this period (it is seen here at nearly twice its actual size). (22, 23, 24)

Intertwined animals decorate the portal of the stave church at Urnes, Norway. This is now reset in the north wall of the church, where it was placed about 1120. At first, however, it formed the central element and doorway of the west end of the original church, which was probably erected c. 1060. These fluid animals of the latest Viking style – named the Urnes style after this church – decorate both the wall planks and the door. (25)

The trappings of death

From a rich grave in the cemetery at Juellinge, on the Danish island of Lolland, comes this female skeleton. On her finger is a gold ring and under her chin, as though clasped by her hand in a drinking position, is an imported Roman sieve. She wore three brooches, and was discovered with two long pins, one on each side of her skull, which presumably fastened a head cloth. The grave dates from the Roman Iron Age. (26)

Imports and influences from the Roman world are a particularly striking element in the Danish archaeological record, although Roman objects are found in Sweden and Norway as well. At the same time, native craftsmen were capable of producing goods of high quality, and some of their techniques were derived from Roman workshops. The bronze vessel above was found in Sweden at Fycklinge, Björksta, Västmanland, in 1819. Originally double-handled, it stands 45 cm high. Also from Sweden is the gold arm-ring (left), found in a bog at Vittskövle, Skåne. The terminals are stylized snakes' heads and the band is beaded along its length. It was probably imported from the south-eastern portion of the Roman Empire. (28, 29)

Imperial and native treasure

Silver and bronze imported
objects (above) come from a
grave at Hoby, Lolland. The jug
(see pl. 3) and large dish, which
portrays Venus between two
cupids, are of bronze. The silver
cups depict scenes from the
Homeric cycle. (31)

Native brooches of silver, inlaid
with impressed gold sheet (right) –
from the Swedish late Roman
Iron Age. The form of the brooch
is basically that of the safety-
pin and ultimately derives from
the European early Iron Age. (32)

Red and black pottery.
The Samian ware (*terra
sigillata*) bowl (left) comes
from a grave at Valloby,
Sjælland, Denmark. This red
pottery is common throughout
the Roman Empire, but is rare
outside its boundaries. A
maker's stamp, 'Comitialis',
dates the bowl to the late
second century. From the same
grave comes the native pottery
(opposite top left), with black
burnished surfaces. (27, 30)

The foundations of wealth

Scandinavian economy was firmly based on agriculture, and farm buildings are impressively large and well built. The reconstructed interior of a farm-house from Tofting, north Germany (left), gives a clear impression of the appearance of many Roman Iron Age houses in Denmark, with living quarters at one end and a byre and storage space at the other. In winter the temperature of the animals' bodies would help to heat the living space. Excavations at the Migration Period site of Vallhagar, Fröjel, Gotland, Sweden (bottom right), produced twenty-four houses. The illustration clearly shows the entrance at each gable and the post-holes for the timbers which supported the roof.

The wealth of the time is demonstrated by the treasure and imported finds. A bronze Campanian situla (below left) was found together with imported Roman bronzes at Havor, Hablingbo, Gotland, Sweden. Also found was a gold neck-ring of south Russian origin, one of the first definite traces of contact with an area which was to become increasingly important to the Swedish economy in the course of the first millennium. The hoard below (centre) is the largest surviving gold treasure of the Migration Period. It comes from Timboholm, Skövde, Västergötland, Sweden, and weighs just over seven kilos (here reproduced at about a third its natural size). (33–36)

Art and ornament

Chip-carving was used to decorate this square-headed brooch (right) from Nordheim, Hedrum, Vestfold. Of mid-fifth-century date, the brooch exhibits some of the earlier features of Style I animal ornament. The highly faceted gilt surface of this object provides a typical example of the method used by Germanic craftsmen throughout Europe in the execution of this early animal style. The head-plate shows the origin of the technique, for similar spiral patterns are found on belt-mounts from late Roman provincial workshops. The form of the brooch was developed in Denmark in the course of the fifth century and gradually spread throughout Europe, reaching its highest standard in Scandinavia and England. (37)

Roman medallions were imitated by Scandinavian craftsmen between the sixth and eighth centuries in the form of impressed gold sheets adapted as pendants, known as bracteates (left). The Roman origin can clearly be seen in the centres of the three upper examples, the main design of which is based on the bust of a Roman emperor. The degeneration of the design is apparent in the largest example where the head takes a messy and slightly misunderstood form. Some of the other bracteates bear designs based on what are presumed to be mythological scenes, or are decorated with animal ornament of normal Migration Period forms. (38)

Precious metals were finely worked in the early fifth
century. Above: the ornamental silver hilts of two
iron swords found in a bog at Kragehul, Fyn,
Denmark, which were presumably deposited as
offerings to the gods after victory. Right: two gold
neck-rings from Skåne in south Sweden testify to the
prosperity of the patron of the arts during this period.
The outer one weighs about 1·5 kilos; the inner one
weighs almost a kilo. Neck-rings and arm-rings of
gold were extremely popular at this time and acted
as a visible indication of wealth. (39, 40)

Daily life
– and death

Who wore these woollen stocking-breeches and shirt, from the great sacrificial bog find (c. 400) at Thorsbjerg in Schleswig? The breeches have slits at the ankle to allow for ease of dressing and there are loops for a belt at the waist. The three wooden implements (middle) are from a tenth-century Swedish boat-burial from Årby, Uppland. They were probably all used at table. Another household item (bottom left) is a loom weight of a typical form used on an upright (warp-weighted) loom. A modern cow's horn has here been used to display mounts, giving an impression of the original appearance of a drinking vessel of a form popular throughout Scandinavia in the first millennium. (41–44)

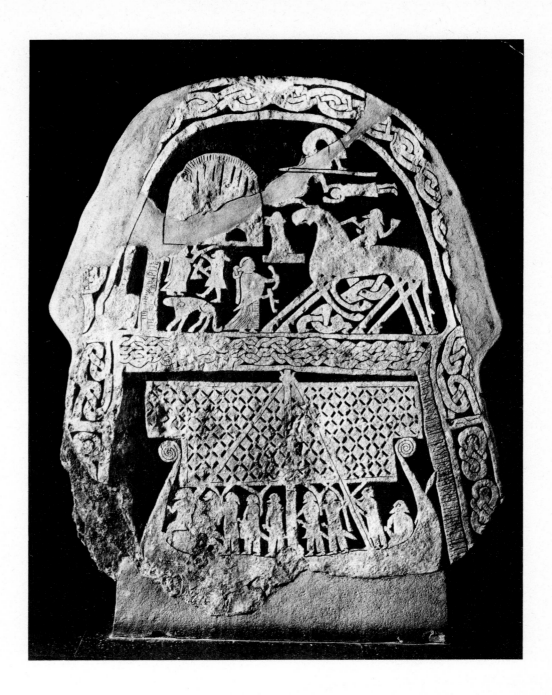

Future life, perhaps, is suggested by one of the great picture stones (above) which abound on the Swedish island of Gotland. Dating from the beginning of the ninth century, this example comes from Tjängvide. The lower field portrays a sailing vessel full of armed warriors. The upper field depicts a building, possibly Valhalla, as well as an eight-legged horse (Sleipnir), whose rider is apparently being greeted by a woman with a drinking-horn. (45)

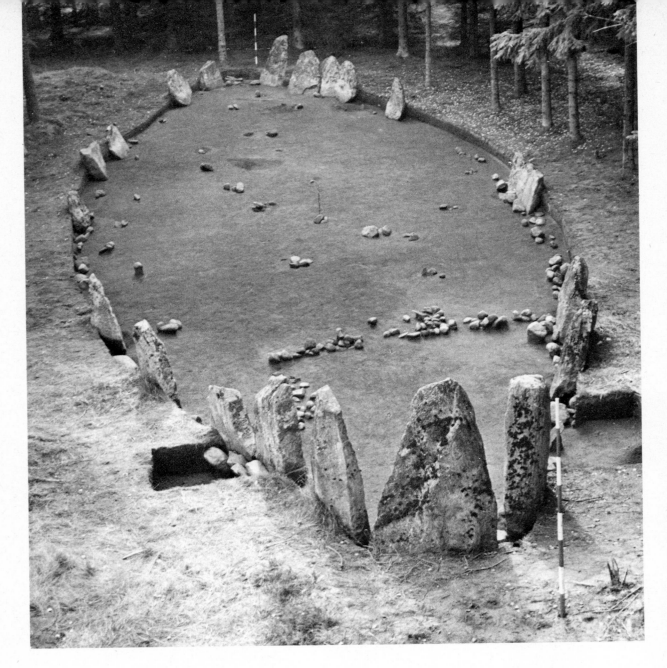

The ship of the dead

Burial in a ship is an idea that has a long history (the ship-setting, left, from Boge, Gotland, almost certainly dates from the late Bronze Age). The example above, however, from Vätteryd, Norra Mellby, Skåne, Sweden, was excavated in 1955 and found to contain much burnt bone, mostly from animals, but also one or two objects which vary widely in date from the Migration Period to the Viking Age. This is but one grave from one of the largest cemeteries of the later Iron Age in south Sweden. Even when some distance from the sea the idea of boat burial was apparently firmly imprinted on men's minds, and was a universal, if somewhat rare, feature of the Scandinavian north. (46,47)

The boat burial at Årby, Uppland (above), was a Swedish Viking Age grave robbed in antiquity. As well as the objects illustrated on p. 40, and some other domestic utensils, an Arab stallion and a greyhound were also laid in the grave. Far away, at Balladoole in the Isle of Man (below), a boat-burial of a Viking settler was laid down in a corner of a pre-existing Christian grave-field within a few hundred metres of the sea. The ship outline of the grave is clearly shown. (48, 49)

The Oseberg ship

Moored, as when at sea, by a rope tied round a great boulder, the most highly decorated vessel yet found (below) comes from Oseberg, Vestfold, Norway. She was preserved in a mound in a reservoir of water formed by the blue clay lining of the trench in which she lay. Within the mound was a young woman, probably a queen, accompanied by a sacrificed slave and a quantity of furniture and equipment (pl. 16) of wood and iron, silver and bronze. Dress, bed-clothes and tapestries were also placed in the chamber built in the centre of the vessel. Most remarkable of the finds were sledges and a wagon (pl. 17) as well as the ship's equipment, some of which is illustrated, left. (50, 51)

Highly sophisticated, the Oseberg ship, found in 1903, is a vessel of the type known as *karfi* (a general-duties vessel), appropriate to a chief in the coastal waters of Norway. Built of oak, she has highly decorated stem- and stern-posts (see pl. 11), and the ornament dates her to *c*. 800. Like all surviving Viking ships she is clinker-built (i.e. her hull planks overlap); she is 21·4 m long and draws about 90 cm of water. She had fifteen pairs of oars, a mast and a square sail. The rudder is laid on the starboard side. Her most striking features are the stem- and stern-posts with their snake-like terminals which coil nearly 5 m above the water-line. Although the posts are not functional, they give an impression of strength and power, an impression perhaps of the dragon-ships referred to in later Scandinavian literature. (52)

The elegant lines of the Gokstad ship make her incomparably the most impressive sailing-vessel to survive from the medieval period. She demonstrates the high standard of the boat-builder's craft in late ninth-century Norway, and her beautiful hull has been copied frequently in recent years in the building of successful and fast replicas for Atlantic crossings. (53, 54)

The Gokstad ship

Excavated in 1880 (left) from a mound about 50 m across, the Gokstad ship (like the Oseberg ship) had been preserved in water in an impermeable blue clay bed. The grave contained a man, perhaps fifty years old, with a great deal of furniture and equipment. Also found in the mound were a number of animals, twelve horses, six dogs and even a peacock. The mound had been robbed in antiquity. (55)

Built of oak, save for the decking, mast, yards and oars, which are of pine, the Gokstad ship measures 23·3 m overall and has a beam of 5·25 m. Her dead weight (unloaded) is about 9 tons (18 tons loaded). Her draught would be between 90 and 95 cm. The prow and stern are incomplete, having rotted away in the grave. The sides are built up of overlapping planks, which were nailed together and then lashed to the frames by means of pliable spruce roots, the two lower strakes being nailed to the keel. The oar holes were closed by wooden covers (top left), which swivelled on a nail. The mast, which might have been as high as 8 or 10 m, could be lowered or raised at will. It carried a yard, to which was attached a square sail. The ship was steered by a large oar attached to the starboard side. She was a remarkably light and elastic boat, which made her ideal in the long Atlantic waves, and she was probably capable of a speed of some 10–12 knots.

Three ship's boats were also found within the mound. Although fragmentary, the two shown below have been convincingly reconstructed. They have rowlocks (left) morticed into their gunwales. (56, 57, 58)

Human sacrifice

At Ballateare in the north of the Isle of Man, excavation produced a well-furnished warrior's grave under a carefully built mound, seen here during excavation (below). The man buried here in the ninth century was apparently a new settler, who ran a large farm. As well as his weapons, he was accompanied to the grave by a number of sacrificed animals (whose burnt bones were scattered over the mound) and by a woman who was buried in the upper part of the mound (on the taller of the two 'shelves' in the picture). Her skull (left) shows the blow that killed her. Proven examples of such human sacrifices are rare in Viking Age contexts. (59, 60)

Grave treasures

From Hejslunds, Hvadhem, Gotland, Sweden, the terminals of a silver arm-ring (left) display remarkable examples of animal heads, which date it a little after 1000. The bronze oval brooches (below) are the commonest type of female ornament of the Viking Age. Made throughout Scandinavia, they survive in great numbers, mostly in graves. Worn in pairs high on the chest, they often supported a festoon of beads made from glass or semi-precious stones. This form of brooch went out of fashion in the early tenth century, to be replaced by disc or ring brooches. (61, 62)

The human image in miniature

A charming reminder of one aspect of the ornament of the Viking Age are these human figures – a contrast to the usual contorted animal motifs of this period, which have a tradition that stretches back to the end of the Roman Iron Age. Used for personal adornment as brooches or pendants, all the figures portrayed here may represent gods, heroes, legends, or whim; but their meaning is lost. The four figures in a row give an impression of female dress in the Viking Age; the long flowing skirt and the short cloak of the lady to the far left are clearly represented, as are

her beads and a ring brooch possibly of Baltic type. The knotted pigtail is frequently encountered on similar brooches and in the scenes portrayed on the picture stones from Gotland. The rider and the man with drawn sword portrayed below presumably represent warriors. The meaning of the pendant, opposite, which clearly dates to about 1000, cannot now be recovered, but it is perhaps not without significance that the man wears a helmet with a nose-guard. All these objects were found in Sweden. (63–66)

To ride and drive

Terrifying head-post from the body of one of the sledges found in the Oseberg ship-burial (the wagon is shown in pl. 17). Clearly intended to frighten the viewer, one might wonder why. Travel over snow was an important factor in the north; movement was swift and sledges and skis must have been in constant use, as were bone skates. A horse was an important and pampered means of transport. Horses of the period, about the size of Icelandic ponies, were fully kitted out with rich gear (bridles, mounts and stirrups, for example, are frequently found in graves). Wooden horse-collars were often richly embellished, as befitted the horse as a draught animal, with mounts like those illustrated opposite, which enrich a tenth-century horse-collar from Søllested, Fyn, Denmark. (67, 68, 69)

Trade and foreign settlement

Scandinavian settlers abroad adapted quickly to the economy and living conditions of their new country, and did not insist on houses like those they had left behind, although in some cases they brought new techniques of building with them. The block houses revealed during the excavations at Staraja Ladoga, in northern Russia, for example (below), are typical local structures of the early Viking Age. Objects found in the excavations, however, show that Scandinavian traders lived here from time to time and controlled some of the trade of this important merchant centre. The settlement of the Atlantic islands demanded different building techniques and materials. At Jarlshof in Shetland (bottom), the incomers took over an existing Pictish settlement and built houses of stone like those that they had known in their homelands. This reconstructed drawing represents the site in the tenth century. (70, 71)

Witness to travels of the Vikings, a marble lion with a runic inscription on its shoulder stands at the entrance to the Arsenal in Venice, brought there by Venetians from the harbour of the Piraeus (the port of Athens). Although the runic inscription is illegible, it nevertheless demonstrates one facet at least of the eastern adventures of the Scandinavians in the Viking Age. (72)

Imports and exports to and from Scandinavia (from top to bottom): twelve iron axes from Gjerrild in Jutland, imported on their spruce stave from Norway (Scandinavia was rich in iron, and iron weapons were much exported); a bronze figure of Buddha, imported from northern India in the late Migration Period to the trading station of Helgö, on Lake Mälar in central Sweden (the eyes are inlaid with silver); a hoard of silver arm-rings from Asarve, Hemse, Gotland, which emphasizes the importance of silver in the Viking economy (it weighs nearly 9 kilos and includes arm-rings from eastern Europe); glass gaming-pieces from Birka, Sweden, probably imported from the East (nine are of dark-green glass, seventeen of blue – the 'King' has decorative threads around the body). (73–76)

Spiritual and temporal power

A fertility god figure, the hammer of Thor, the Sign of Christ on the Cross (opposite) and a scene from the Oseberg wagon (opposite below) bring us near to the spiritual and religious beliefs of the Vikings. Only with Christianity, however, do we grasp the true significance of such objects; many have tried to interpret the meaning of the Oseberg scene, but with no success. (77–80)

Spear, sword, axe, shield and helmet were the prestigious weapons of the Germanic world. Most important of these was the sword, a weapon owned by the few, rather than the many. The professional Viking soldier would have had a sword about 92 cm long with a hilt like that (right) from Sørup, near Løgstør, Jutland, Denmark. The pommel and guard in this case are decorated with brass plates cast with a geometrical design. The tang would be covered with wood and leather. The blade would be two-edged with a rounded tip, demonstrating the sword's use as a slashing weapon in combat.

A warrior of the Viking Period is depicted (below) on the tip of an antler tine found at Sigtuna, Sweden. He wears a conical helmet with a nose-guard (the only real parallel is a Viking helmet in Budapest). As with so many representations of men in the Viking Age he has a moustache and neatly dressed hair, far from the shaggy vision so often portrayed in popular modern drawings. (81, 82)

Fortification

Fortified encampment was a familiar idea in Scandinavia from the early Iron Age onwards. There are hundreds of forts in Sweden alone, some of which have been used and reused throughout the ages. Left: the fortification at Ismantorp, Långlöt, Öland, is about 125 m in diameter and has nine gates in its massive wall, which stands to a height of 4 m. It is generally held that the camp was built at the end of the Roman Iron Age or in the early Migration Period. Below: the fortified settlement of Eketorp, Gräsgård, on the southern tip of the same island, is clearly closely related to Ismantorp in plan. This photo was taken during the excavations and shows the line of the outer palisade outside the main bank. The houses which can be seen belong to the second phase of settlement, which is dated 400–700. The earliest fortification was planted c. 300; it was again inhabited in the late Viking Age, c. 1100, and settlement continued into the thirteenth century. (83, 84)

Harald Bluetooth planned to consolidate the Danish Kingdom in the middle of the tenth century, and he seems to have initiated a policy of public works, chief among which was defence. It was probably he who fortified Hedeby (bottom), the most southerly town in his kingdom, building a great bank and palisade (here seen from the air). The bank enclosed this important merchant centre and protected it from attack by Saxons or Slavs from the south.

The circular Slav fortified settlements of eastern Europe may indeed have inspired him to build the great series of fortifications of the Trelleborg type (that from Trelleborg, Sjælland, is reconstructed below). Four of these fortresses are known and their function is much discussed. They were all laid out with great attention to geometry in very similar circumstances and at the same period. They were not simply barracks, rather they must be seen in another defensive function; perhaps as royal strong-points set up partly to control, partly to protect, the inhabitants of the surrounding countryside. (85, 86)

The law-makers meet

The great assembly of the Icelandic people (the Althing), held annually at Thingvellir, as portrayed by the scholar-artist W. G. Collingwood. It was here that disputes were settled, laws agreed, policy discussed and bargains made. Here, in 1000, Christianity was accepted by democratic decision as the religion of this new colony in the north. (87)

ᚠᚢᚦᚨᚱᚲᚷᚹ ᚺᚾᛁᛃᛈᛇᛉᛊ ᛏᛒᛖᛗᛚᛜᛞᛟ

fuþarkgw h nijpeRs tbemlngd o

Memorials in stone

Not illiterate, as frequently regarded, the Scandinavians of the period covered by this book had a script (opposite top) which had been invented somewhere in the Germanic world for carving on wood (hence the characters are angular to make it easy to carve across the grain). Few normal messages of Viking Age date or earlier survive (although a very large group of medieval inscriptions of normal everyday character have been found in the medieval levels of the Norwegian town of Bergen). Most of the Viking Age runes occur on stones raised either to commemorate a man's death or his good works. They tell of ventures in trade, of warfare and raids, of the peaceful work of the farming community, of the deeds of men and of the religion of the inhabitants of the Scandinavian countries. They are also important documents in the study of the history of late Viking Age ornament and literature, as shown by an inscription carved on a boulder from Ed, Uppland, Sweden (opposite centre and left) in memory of a man who had been 'leader of the host' in the Byzantine Empire. A stone from Sjusta, Skokloster, Uppland, (opposite right), records the death of four sons of Runa, a widow, one of whom had died in Novgorod. A stone from Busby, Täby, Uppland (right), tells of a man called Östen who went to Jerusalem and died in Greece. All the inscriptions illustrated here are of eleventh-century date. (88–92)

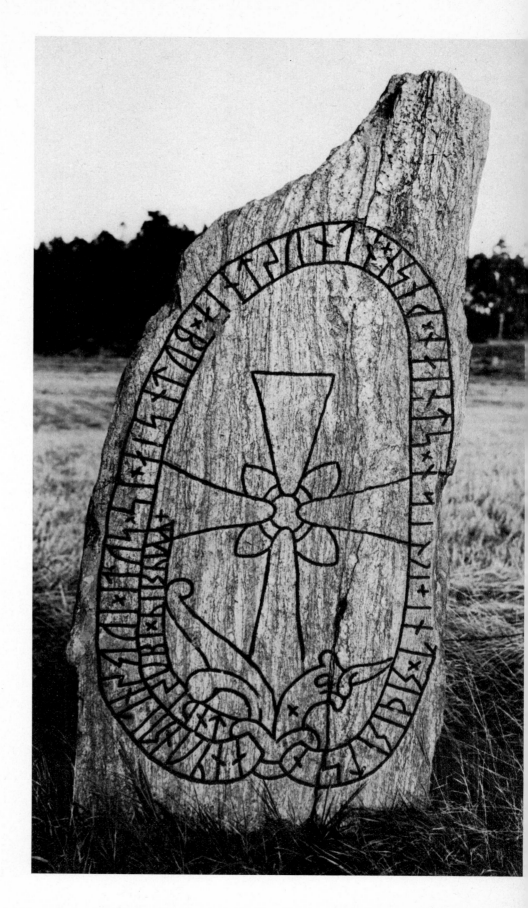

Standing stone cross in the churchyard at Gosforth, Cumberland – it is the largest surviving piece of sculpture from pre-Norman England. It was probably carved between 900 and 930 and includes scenes from both Christian and pagan religious cycles. The crucifixion which appears on one face is contrasted with pagan scenes on the other side. The interlace work is executed in the Borre style, one of the most popular Scandinavian styles to be introduced into England and one which was particularly favoured in the Irish Sea region. (93)

2 The era of the great migrations

Throughout the first millennium, Europe had some of the qualities of a maelstrom: the tribes of Europe were on the move, searching for richer land, fleeing from tyranny, seeking booty or *Lebensraum*. Although Scandinavia was on the edge of this disturbance, it was responsible for some of it. It was from Denmark that the Angles and Jutes moved to conquer and settle in the British Isles; legend would have it that the Goths and Burgundians also had their origin in Scandinavia, but of this there is no direct evidence. With the collapse of the Roman Empire the movements became almost frenetic; Huns, Goths, Vandals, wave upon wave of tribes, moved across Europe, giving momentum to the peoples of the Continent. This restless epoch – the Migration Period – lasted until the rise of Charlemagne, the crystallization of the main European states, and the coming of the Vikings in the late eighth century.

There are few historical sources for Scandinavia in the Migration Period, all that survive are incidental references in Mediterranean, Frankish and Anglo-Saxon sources, often little more than a reference to a tribe or its chief. Certain episodes in Scandinavian history are hinted at, but no consecutive story is revealed; only a rather shadowy impression of an area racked by internecine war – as the Svíar of Uppland, for instance, attempted to gain control of Sweden, as the Danes fought the Norwegians, as Frisia was raided by Swedes. Once again archaeology is the key to an understanding of the period where historical sources are slender, contradictory and almost legend.

In the greater part of Scandinavia this was a wealthy period, and, although times were troubled, the people of the northern countries appear to have increased in political and economic stature, perhaps because of the comparative stability of their economy and the absence of serious threat from outside their borders. Although never free from internal trouble – as many a violently destroyed farm dramatically relates in the archaeological record – the Scandinavians were building up a self-confident civilization of their own between 400 and 800, which was largely independent of outside influence and which reached its full-blooded maturity with the Viking adventure. The seeds of this adventure were sown in these four hundred years and the harvest was gathered in between 800 and 1100. In Sweden the Migration Period, and the period of two hundred years before the Viking adventure began (the Vendel Period), has been described as an age of gold. Some of the plunder of Europe seems to have rubbed off on their fingers: a gold hoard found at Tureholm in Södermanland in 1774 weighed some 12 kilos, and another from Timboholm in Västergötland weighed 7 kilos.

Scandinavia was rich, and in no place is this better seen than in the graves of the wealthy families of Sweden. Considerable mounds were erected over the dead and bodies were sometimes placed in a ship which was then covered by an earthen mound. In certain cases, mostly in the early Viking Age, the burial was surrounded by a setting of stones in the form of a ship, with taller stones at each end to represent the rising prow and stern-post of a real vessel. The association of the ship with death has deep roots (in Scandinavia there is evidence of some such belief as early as the Bronze Age); the idea of a voyage on the uncharted seas of death is natural to any seafaring man, and we may perhaps peep into the mind of the period through the words of an Anglo-Saxon poet who was describing a Scandinavian chieftain's funeral. Although in this description from the epic poem *Beowulf* the ship is not buried in a mound, the idea which lies behind it would be familiar to the Scandinavian of the Migration, Vendel or Viking Period who buried his chieftain with great state:

> There at the quay, stood a ring-prowed ship –
> The radiant and eager ship of the lord.
> They laid down the beloved lord,
> The giver of rings, in the bosom of the ship,
> The lord lay by the mast. They brought from afar
> Many great treasures and costly trappings.
> I never heard of a ship so richly furnished as this,
> With weapons of war, armour of battle,
> Swords and corslets. Many treasures lay
> Piled on his breast.

Such ships were uncovered during the excavation of two great cemeteries in Uppland – at Vendel and Valsgärde – but other ship burials of almost equal wealth have also been recorded from other parts of Scandinavia, from Lackalänge in Skåne for example. The graves of the fifth and sixth centuries had been plundered at Valsgärde – a feature noted elsewhere in Sweden – and only seventh-and eighth-century graves survive. An idea of the impressive nature of the earlier graves can be gained from the royal cemetery at Old Uppsala, a short distance from the modern town of Uppsala. The four largest mounds form part of a large cemetery and are set in line on a ridge. The westernmost is the largest, some 12 m high, and is only surpassed in height by one other Swedish mound, *Anund's* mound in Badelunda, Västmanland, although the great Norwegian mound in Romerike, known as Raknehaugen, is 95 m in diameter and 19 m high. The finds from the three excavated Uppsala mounds are disappointing, but they do enable us to confirm the dating of these graves to the Migration Period and to indentify the dynasty and even possibly the kings who were buried here. From both Norse and Anglo-Saxon sources we have evidence of a royal family known as the Ynglingr; one king, Egil, is said in these sources to have been buried beneath a mound at Uppsala. Intelligent guess-work would suggest that three of the princes buried beneath these great mounds were Aun, Egil and Adils, all of whom appear in *Ynglinga-saga*. A fourth prince, Ottar, was perhaps buried a few miles away in a mound already known by his name at the end of the seventeenth century. Old Uppsala was also an important cult centre and the site of a temple, details of which are recorded by Adam of Bremen.

The aristocratic Swedish cemeteries at Vendel and Valsgärde have yielded a series of rich burials which extend from the Migration Period into the Viking Period. As we have seen, many of the dead were buried in boats and with them were found richly ornamented swords, elaborate helmets, bridle mounts, shields, embellished with highly ornamented bosses and charges, brooches, glass and more everyday objects such as tools, combs and vessels. Not only were inanimate objects laid in the graves, but the boats and their occupants were sometimes accompanied by horses – often more than one – which were placed alongside, in the trench built to receive the ship. The burials at Vendel and Valsgärde can only be considered as the burials of chieftains, for no other class of society could have borne the capital expenditure involved in the sacrifice of these costly treasures. The lavishness of the burials gives a remarkable impression not only of the wealth of the family, but also of the solidly based economy of middle Sweden.

Grave-finds of similar richness have not yet been found in either Denmark or Norway, but some cemeteries in these countries reflect an only slightly less wealthy society. Lousgård, on the Danish island of Bornholm, provided a burial-place for a rich aristocratic family, at least one member of which was accompanied to the grave by a sacrificed slave. The fine graves at Snartemo, Vest Agder, provide a Norwegian parallel. Here again can be seen abundant wealth: rich weapons, glass vessels, bronze bowls, gold rings as well as humbler objects.

The great hoards which were mentioned at the beginning of this chapter are symptomatic of a period of trouble and war. Hoards tend to be buried in time of danger, and the fact that they are found today and were never reclaimed indicates that the fear of the original owners was not misplaced. The hoards chiefly belong to the fifth and early sixth centuries and represent bullion – the portable wealth of a family or person. Many of the objects they contain are unornamented rings and spirals made of plain gold bands, and such things may well have been made to some sort of standard of weight; other objects have great beauty and are extremely skilfully made. The great neck-rings of Sweden, for example, are among the most perfect pieces of European jewellery of the period. One hoard symbolizes the wealth of this period and provides one of the most romantic and popular stories of Danish archaeology. The two golden horns from Gallehus were made at the period of transition from the Roman Iron Age to the Migration Period. The first was found in 1639 and the second in 1734 in the same field at Tønder, South Jutland. They were stolen from the Royal Collection in Copenhagen in 1802 and melted down by the thief before he was caught. We know them now only through contemporary drawings and a reconstruction made soon after their loss. The saddest aspect of this story is that copies were made for presentation before the theft, but none of them can now be traced, one copy indeed was lost at sea off Corsica on its way to join the collection of Cardinal Stephen Borgia. The horns consisted of a plain inner shell and an outer shell made up of several cylinders; one was 82·5 cm long, the other 52·5 cm. One bore a runic inscription which may be translated: 'I Hlégestr of Holt [?] made the horn'. They were decorated with applied and engraved figures, which presumably had mythological significance, as well as animal ornament of a type which we will consider below.

The gold coins – *solidi* from the Mediterranean – found so frequently in the hoards indicate the ultimate source of the metal and perhaps even of the wealth of these people. The trade which had grown during the Roman Iron Age continued through the succeeding periods and, as quality luxury goods became rarer in southern Europe and as the Scandinavians developed a refined and distinctive taste of their own, gold became one of the most desirable of all imports. Despite the occasional occurrence of luxury goods, such as glass, in the graves, it is perhaps significant that a common find in the richer graves – as at Snartemo – is a pair of scales, sometimes with weights, which was presumably used for weighing precious metals in the course of mercantile transactions. The natural wealth of the North continued to provide a surplus for export.

Wealth and trade, loot and war

67

It is during this period that we find the first settlement which can properly be called a trading post. It is hardly a town; but Helgö, an island in Lake Mälar not very far from Stockholm in the centre of what was once a kingdom of the Svíar, is the first settlement in Scandinavia that can be recognized as not having had a primarily agricultural or military basis. Excavation since 1954 has revealed a series of houses set either on terraces on the rocky slopes above the shore or on the flatter low-lying shore itself. Apparently founded in the fifth century, it began to lose its importance in the late eighth century, when the nearby town of Birka began to dominate the area. Excavation has not yet revealed the full extent of the site nor all the implications of its enormous importance, but the results so far reveal an economic unit of considerable significance. Imported goods of glass, metalwork and pottery reveal connections with Western Europe and the Mediterranean, as well as with Poland, Finland and the Baltic states. Perhaps the most incredible object symbolizing such connections is the sixth- or seventh-century bronze figure of a Buddha which, presumably through many intermediate hands, reached Sweden from the valleys of northern India, from Kashmir or Afghanistan. Helgö was also a centre of industry, producing among other things a vast quantity of cheap jewellery cast in bronze from clay moulds found in great abundance in one area of the site; there is, moreover, evidence of ironworking and various other crafts.

But the times were troubled. At Sorte Muld and Dalshøj in Bornholm, for example farms were burnt down and, as a grim reminder of the fate of the people who were buried there, hoards are found in the vicinity of the buildings. The inhabitants had not been protected by a nearby encampment which they had built in the neighbourhood against just such an eventuality. This attack in the early sixth century came at much the same time as similar troubles in the Swedish offshore island of Gotland. Professor Stenberger has demonstrated, by a study of the coins found in them, that the deposition of hoards in the Baltic islands took place during relatively short periods. The hoards on Öland were probably laid down between 480 and 490, while on Gotland they were deposited between 500 and 520. On both islands traces are found of destroyed settlements at about this time.

This was, therefore, a period when defence was an important element in the lives of the Scandinavians of the Baltic, and large numbers of forts or strongholds were built in areas which were easily accessible to raiders from the sea. Many of these forts must have been built during the Migration Period as temporary refuges to which people fled in time of sudden invasion by pirates or politically inspired raiders. They were usually set on eminences, sometimes far from the coast, sometimes far from arable land, and in time of trouble a man would retreat to them with his family, his livestock and his portable treasure. The island of Öland provides the most dramatic example of such a refuge: among some rather modest enclosures are two fantastic circular fortifications, which were used over a very long period. These sites – Gråborg and Ismantorp – are set in the barren central limestone region of this island, far from the coast and from arable land. The largest is Gråborg which is about 200 m in diameter and was used intermittently over a period of a thousand years, being refortified in the late Middle Ages. Throughout the island the ruins of abandoned farms of this period demonstrate the need for these forts.

In at least one place a community tried to fortify itself permanently from such inroads. Professor Mårten Stenberger has, since 1964, been excavating a fortified site – Eketorp – on the edge of the barren limestone region of central Öland almost at the southern tip of the island. The fort is circular, 80 m in diameter, and surrounded by a bank of stone, which may originally have been about 6 m high; 10 m from the wall a timbered palisade gave additional protection to the stronghold. The place was inhabited between about 450 and 700/750 and again between the beginning of the eleventh and the end of the thirteenth century; it was probably deserted between these two periods. Finds indicate that Eketorp was a permanent settlement whose occupants pursued the normal economic course of an agricultural community, cultivating the fields around the edge of the nearby lake and raising stock, brewing beer and supporting certain local craftsmen, such as a smith. A few imported objects – particularly glass – suggest a reasonably good economy as does a small hoard of gold. Eketorp, however, is an important – if, as far as we know at present, atypical – phenomenon in the northern countries, as it is the first known permanently inhabited Scandinavian fortification. It provides evidence of a close-knit community, living in houses with party walls set radially around the edge of the circle formed by the defending bank of the settlement. There were probably about forty such buildings round this circle; not all were dwelling-houses (some were byres and store-houses), but they were all constructed in the same fashion: they had foundations of stone, and these were probably crowned by turf walls and roofed with turf supported by a row of central posts. The plan of the Ismantorp fort is similar, but trial excavations have shown this to be empty of settlement material. This led to the previously held belief that these forts were temporary refuges; now that Eketorp has belied this, perhaps we shall have to reconsider the function of other sites.

A cause and a consequence of the newly found riches of the Scandinavian people was the settlement of new territory on the basis of a new economy, an economy designed to produce goods for trade to the south. In search of furs, iron, horn and ivory the Norwegians and Swedes turned to the North. In the greater part of northern Scandinavia there had lived since the Stone Age a people whose economy was based on hunting, and fishing, where the chief tools were made of bone and stone and where iron and bronze were luxuries. In the northern provinces of Norway and Sweden, from the beginning of the Vendel Period, we begin to find graves and casual types of evidence which demonstrate a movement by the Swedes towards the Norwegian border along the river valleys leading to the rich north-west coast of Norway. At the same time the search for wealth caused the settlement of many of the non-arable districts of Norway by expansion along the coast and into the fjords and mountains: settlement sites indicate an interest in stock-breeding, hunting and iron extraction. That these specialist industries were successful is obvious from the rich character of the graves of the area.

New land and homeland

In the original homelands there is much evidence of settlement and houses. The destruction of many settlements in the Baltic islands provides a unique opportunity to study the houses of the period between 400 and 600. The foundations of some 2,300 large rectangular houses of this period have been discovered in the islands of Öland and Gotland alone. They vary in length between 5 m and 60 m and are usually grouped together as three or four structures loosely related to other houses in similar groups. Such groups are surrounded by a farmyard of which the crumbling walls often survive.

Vallhagar on Gotland is the best known of these settlements. Excavation has revealed some five or six farms comprising some twenty-four buildings and three grave-fields. The Vallhagar houses are typical of all the Gotland buildings of this period. Each house had limestone wall foundations, and the roof, which may have been of turf or reeds, was supported on a double row of posts. Entrances were usually placed at the gable-ends and there was a hearth on the main axis. In two cases the houses were like those recorded in the Roman Iron Age in Denmark, where the living quarters were at one end and a byre was screened off at the other end. Among the finds analysed was grain; oats were not found, but barley was recovered and wheat and rye also occurred. Sheep and cattle bones were found in proportion of about 2:1, pigs as well as horses were also kept.

Similar types of houses and even settlements occur in Denmark and Norway. A strange form of Norwegian barrack-like settlement is typified by that at Lekskaren in Rogaland, and is found only in this area (round Stavanger) and in northern Norway. Such settlements usually consist of a series of long houses ranged so that their gable-ends face an open central space. The lack of definite byre-like buildings and associated field complexes might suggest that they were refuges equivalent to the forts of Öland, or that they were merchants' winter quarters. Their date is by no means certain.

Art and decoration

A rare occurrence of naturalism in the art of this period is this animal, scratched on the back of a sixth-century square-headed brooch from Nordheim, Hedrum, Vestfold, Norway (see pl. 37). Typically, it is found casually placed on an otherwise formally decorated object.

During this period of wealth and expansion the peoples of Scandinavia were becoming conscious of their own taste. One of the most remarkable expressions of this self-confidence is seen in their art, for it was during the last stages of the Roman Iron Age and the beginning of the Migration Period that there developed in Scandinavia the beginnings of an art which in one of its aspects at least – animal ornament – was to continue in an unbroken tradition until the end of the Viking Age. Two separate forms of ornament spanned this period: a naturalistic art of surprising quality and sensitivity and an abstract art of striking originality and extreme tortuousness. It is hard to evaluate the naturalistic art as so little of it survives, but where it is encountered its assured quality demonstrates that this was a rich vein in the art of the North and one would wish to see more of it. Instead we are presented with an intimate and sophisticated abstract art, individual but brilliant and not to everyone's taste; it is an applied art, appearing almost exclusively as an embellishment on objects of daily use. It is seen on brooches and swords, on pendants and helmets, it appears on metal and it appears on stone. Wood must also have been used, but, although this would be the natural medium for the Scandinavian artist, no major piece of decorative art can be seen in this medium until the beginning of the Viking Age. The art is remarkable, its elements tease our vision and often degenerate into patterns the meaning of which can only be recognized by the trained eye. It is related to the art of northern Europe, to the art of all the Germanic people and was apparently impervious to the more formal ornament of the Mediterranean with its emphasis on naturalism.

The main element of this abstract art is a semi-naturalistic animal ornament which has its roots in the late Roman Iron Age, when animal designs based on Romano-Germanic originals occur on objects made in Scandinavia. These objects are mostly made of impressed metal, but the introduction of a new technique, derived from the provincial Roman repertoire, changed these semi-naturalistic creatures into much more elaborate forms. This technique was chip-carving, a method of cutting a flat surface with the corner of a chisel into a series of facets so

70

that the objects would glitter in any light; it was adapted from woodworking to jewellery and appears in silver and bronze, metals which were often gilded or inlaid with niello – the black sulphide of silver.

More than seventy years ago a Swedish archaeologist, Bernhard Salin, divided the art of the period from 400 to 900 into Styles I, II, and III. Although this system has been modified by the recognition of many sub-styles, it still holds good in the main and can appropriately be used here. The art of Style I is based on a contorted, multi-faceted single animal. Between the time when this animal appears, towards the end of the fifth century, and the period when it is replaced by the Style II animal, a hundred or so years later, it becomes more distorted and degenerate until it reaches a stage where it is almost unrecognizable.

An interesting sidelight is thrown on the origin of this style if we examine the series of impressed gold circular pendants, known as bracteates, which are found in some quantity in Scandinavia. These pendants bear a design which is based on the profile portrait of a Roman emperor of the type found on coins and medallions. This motif is subsequently adapted and changed until the head becomes grotesque. Ultimately the bust disappears completely and it replaced by Style I ornament. We can see here an expression of the Scandinavian abhorrence of the naturalistic in its applied art.

At the end of the sixth century Style II was introduced into Scandinavia from southern Europe and captured the imagination of the inhabitants, who became fascinated by it and raised it to the heights of its expression in the rich graves of Vendel and Valsgärde. Style II is based on inter-laced animals of ribbon-like form, and the slow curves of this style, executed in chip-carved gilt bronze, appeared in a variety of forms to delight the eye of the Scandinavian until the end of the eighth century, when it was absorbed and changed into the more fussy art of the Viking Period. It was this style which, towards the beginning of the Viking era, fined into the rather more complicated Style III, the first truly Viking style.

The development of the early animal style: a detail (left) of the fragmentary square-headed brooch from Langlo, Stokke, Vestfold, Norway, shows a reasonably logical example of a Style I animal. The treatment of the human figure (centre) demonstrates the body split up into its component parts and already beginning to lose some of its logicality (from the Snartemo sword, reverse side, pl. 1). On the right, a classic Style II type animal (on a belt-mount from grave XII at Vendel) exemplifies the sinuous characteristics and articulated nature of the newly introduced art of the seventh century.

Map of sites mentioned in the text.

Norway:
1 Sætrang, 2 Kvalsund,
3 Raknehaugen,
4 Snartemo,
5 Gokstad, 6 Oseberg,
7 Tune, 8 Asker,
9 Kaupang,
10 Borre, 11 Urnes.

Denmark:
12 Hoby, 13 Himmlingøje,
14 Nørre Fjand, 15 Dalshøj,
16 Ginderup, 17 Nydam,
18 Vimose, 19 Ejsbøl,
20 Kragehul, 21 Thorsbjerg,
22 Illerup, 23 Lousgård, 24 Sorte Muld, 25 Lindholm,
26 Trelleborg, 27 Fyrkat,
28 Aggersborg, 29 Jelling.

Sweden:
30 Fycklinge, 31 Hablingbo,
32 Moos, 33 Kylver,
34 Käringsjön, 35 Skedemosse,
36 Timboholm, 37 Vendel,
38 Valsgärde, 39 Lackalänge,
40 Helgö, 41 Birka, 42 Gråborg,
43 Ismantorp, 44 Eketorp,
45 Vallhagar, 46 Galtabäck,
47 Falsterbo, 48 Västergarn.

Germany:
49 Hedeby.

Latvia:
50 Grobin.

3 The Viking attack

In a word, although there were an hundred hard-steeled iron heads on one neck, and an hundred sharp, ready, cool, never rusting, brazen tongues in each head, and an hundred garrulous, loud, unceasing voices from each tongue, they could not recount or narrate, enumerate or tell, what all the Irish suffered in common, both men and women, laity and clergy, old and young, noble and ignoble, of hardships and of injuring and of oppression, in every house, from those valiant, wrathful, purely pagan people.

This hyperbolic passage from an Irish writer of the twelfth century summarizes the impression which the Vikings made on the Western European mind. Wild statements of this sort have coloured all discussion of the great Viking adventure which brought Scandinavia for the first time into political contact with the rest of the known world. The story which is to be told in this chapter concerns the gradual rise of an empire which, at the beginning of the eleventh century, stretched in theory from North Cape to the Isles of Scilly and admitted a Scandinavian king as an equal to his brothers in the rest of Christendom. It is the story of voyages of exploration, to Iceland, Greenland and America, of merchant journeys into the heart of Asia and of theft and rapine in the Western Isles.

In Western Europe the Viking activities are well documented, and if the clerical chroniclers tend to become rather hysterical about the Viking progress they apparently had some reason. The first Viking raid is recorded dramatically under the year 793 in the *Anglo-Saxon Chronicle*:

In Britain and Western Europe

> In this year dire portents appeared over Northumbria and sorely frightened the people. They consisted of immense whirlwinds and flashes of lightning, and fiery dragons were seen flying in the air. A great famine immediately followed these signs, and a little after that . . . on 8th June, the ravages of heathen men miserably destroyed God's church of Lindisfarne with plunder and slaughter.

This is the first of many references of like character to the raiding activities of the pagan Scandinavians: references scattered in the pages of chroniclers and letter-writers throughout Europe. In 851 the Scandinavians (now formed into an army) spent their first winter in England, in 865 they took the Danegeld (a vast political bribe) for the first time, while in 867 the character of the raids changed when Halfdan seized York and finally settled in 876 in the old English kingdom of Northumbria. Finally in 886 the treaty of Alfred with Guthrum gave to the Scandinavians the right to settle in the north of England and in the area soon to be known as the Five Boroughs – Nottingham, Lincoln, Stamford, Derby, and Leicester. The Vikings ruled these areas in their own right and incursions from Dublin and Norway added the north-west of England to their area of influence in the early tenth century. York became an important centre of the Scandinavians in the west. Here they founded and maintained, until 954, a major trading station in a town with Roman origins. Excavation in the 1960s and 70s has revealed a great deal of physical evidence of their presence there and of the industries that flourished there. So important was the mercantile power of the Scandinavians that, long after the last Danish king had been expelled from the city, merchants from the other side of the North Sea were a major element in the economic life of the community. By the middle of the tenth century, all these areas were nominally back under English control and it was not until early in the next century that Scandinavian kings, after a series of major military incursions, reigned again in England. The eleventh-century Viking conquest was of a different type, a conquest carried out for political aggrandizement and an increase of royal revenue.

These incursions have left traces in the archaeological record. Coin hoards and a handful of pagan-style burials tell of the troubled state of England up to the time of Halfdan's settlement and Alfred's treaty, while Christian memorials in the Scandinavian taste and Viking elements in the art tell of the reconciliation of two cultures. More striking perhaps is the evidence of the place-names. In the East Riding of Yorkshire for example, 40 per cent of the place-names recorded in Domesday Book are of Scandinavian origin; in the North Riding, 38 per cent; in the West Riding only between 13 and 19 per cent. Even the names of some towns were changed: *Northworthig*, for example, became Derby. But many villages and towns retained their old names, although the Viking presence is attested by graves or memorials in the Viking taste. Although the point is disputed it seems on this evidence that there was a considerable population incursion into England in the ninth century. The raids and subsequent events can also be traced in Scandinavia. In a few Viking graves in Norway, for example, are fragments of Anglo-Saxon metalwork adapted as ornaments by the men and women of the North – some, at least, rudely torn from their original settings on books and shrines. In Sweden nearly 34,000 Anglo-Saxon coins in the great hoards of the tenth and eleventh centuries reflect the Danegeld – the tax paid by the English to their conquerors, a tax which is sometimes recorded on runic memorial stones to Viking warriors, as at Yttergärde in Uppland, Sweden, where a stone was erected by Karse and Karlbjörn in memory of their father Ulv of Borresta: 'And Ulv has taken three gelds in England. That was the first that Tosti paid, then Thorkel paid, then Cnut paid.' The rune-stones tell us more of these attacks, personalizing the attackers in the time of Cnut, as for example on the Nävelsjö stone from the Swedish province of Småland: 'Gunnkel set this stone in memory of Gunnar his father, Rode's son. Helgi laid him in a stone coffin in England in Bath.'

England was not the only Western European country to receive attention from the Vikings. The Faroe Isles, northern Scotland, the Scottish Isles, the Isle of Man and Ireland were all settled by the Vikings. Viking kings and chiefs proliferated and founded such towns as Dublin, Cork and Limerick to further their trade and act as bases for piratical attacks which they mounted on both England and the Continent (the north-west of England was largely settled by Norwegians based on Dublin and Man). The Low Countries and France did not escape the Viking incursions; between 841 and 844 Quentovic, Rouen and Nantes were attacked and ruthlessly sacked. The great port of Dorestad at the mouth of the Rhine was for some time controlled by a Viking, Rorik, who was virtually the ruler of the Low Countries. Paris and Trier were attacked and in 911 the Norwegians settled Normandy. Spain was raided in the mid-ninth century; indeed the whole of the western seaboard of Europe and towns on many of the major river entries into the Continent received the attention of Vikings in search of plunder and booty.

Possibly the greatest adventures of the Vikings in the West were in the Atlantic, where they discovered new lands – Iceland, Greenland, and North America. According to Ari the Wise, writing about 1130, Iceland was inhabited by Irish monks before the Vikings arrived in the late ninth century. No archaeological trace of these inhabitants has yet been discovered, but it seems likely that Iceland was known to the Vikings before the traditional date of 860 for the first three Viking voyages of exploration by a Swede, Gardar Svavarson, and two Norwegians, Naddod and Flokki Vilgerdason. The land-hungry Vikings liked what they saw; indeed one of Flokki's party reported that every blade of grass dripped with butter – a judgment which is difficult to understand when one considers the colours of this bleak and practically treeless country. About ten years later the settlement of Iceland began. Ari, in his history the *Íslendingabók*, tells of this settlement:

> Iceland was first settled from Norway in the days of Harald Fairhair, son of Halfdan the Black according to the opinion and calculation of Teit my foster-father . . . and of my paternal uncle Thorkel Gellisson who remembered far back, and of Thurid daughter of Snorri the *goði* who was both learned in many things and trustworthy . . . 870 years after the birth of Christ.

> A Norwegian called Ingólf, it is reliably reported, first went thence to Iceland when Harald Fairhair was sixteen winters old, and for the second time a few winters later. He settled south in Reykjarvík. It is called Ingólfshöfði [Ingólf's Head], east of Minþakseyri, where he made his first landing, and Ingólfsfell, west of Ölfossá, where he took possession of land.

In the course of the next fifty or sixty years all the suitable land had been taken. *Landnámabók* gives the names of about four hundred of the chief settlers, but many more people must have come into the country – thirty-five of these settlers, for instance, came, it is explicitly stated, in their own ships. It has been calculated that by the middle of the tenth century between three thousand and four thousand families, representing perhaps some fifty thousand to sixty thousand people, were living in the country. On the basis of the literary sources we can say that about half of them came from the area round the present-day town of Bergen in Norway – the area of the *Gulatingslag* – and were apparently fleeing from the tyranny of Harald Fairhair who was trying to establish his authority in western Norway. Others came from other parts of Scandinavia and many from the Viking areas of Britain. In Iceland was established a republic of semi-aristocratic character, at first ruled over by the secular priests (*goði*), thirty-two of whom became in 930 the first members of the consultative assembly – the Althing – with one of their number Úlfljót as *Lögsögumaðr* (law speaker or chairman). The Althing (backed by a series of local assemblies) met each summer at Thingvellir not far from Reykjavík and fulfilled many purposes: as a court for promulgating the law, as a fair and as a social occasion. Over the years its character changed and its numbers grew until the Norwegian king, Hákon Hákonsson, took control of Iceland in 1262–4. In this rich country with its teeming rivers, flocks of tender sea-birds, good pasture, its seals and whales, a strong society grew up whose doings are recorded in sagas and other tales which have their roots in the tenth and eleventh centuries, but were not written down until the thirteenth century. These stories are great literature; the best – the sagas of Njal, Egil and the Laxdalers, for example – are exciting and fascinating reading to this day; they and the splendid poetry of the late tenth century open a window into the history of Iceland and, more important, into the minds of the people who settled this vast land a thousand years ago. The sagas need careful sifting if we are to draw history from them, but it is through them that Iceland's claim to have contributed to the European cultural heritage is most successfully made.

From Iceland to Greenland, across the Denmark Strait, is no great distance, and it was not long before the settlers of Iceland discovered this forbidding and gloomy land with its inhospitable coastline penetrated on the western side of the country by deep fjords. The man who is credited with the settlement of Greenland was called Erik the Red, and he came from Jaeder in Norway, having had to leave in a hurry, 'because of some killings.' He got into trouble in Iceland and, about 980, was outlawed. He determined to go in search of a land which a storm-tossed Icelander called Gunnbjörn Ulf-Krakason had seen, but not landed on, some fifty years earlier. Erik rounded Cape Farewell and spent three years in exploring the land between Herjolfsnes (Ikigait) and Eiriksfjord (Tunugdliarfik). He named the country Greenland and, having sailed back to Iceland, where he ran into more trouble, he decided to settle the new land. He returned to Greenland with a group of followers who increased in numbers over the years. Two main settlements were founded: one, centred on Erik's farm at Brattahlid (Qagssiarssuk) in Eiriksfjord, was known as the Eastern settlement; the other, further north, round the modern Godthåb, was known as the Western settlement. The land was rich in wild life, in seals, in fish, whales and sea-birds; there was a little pasture and, as long as the fur and walrus ivory could be exported to Europe, the future of the new land was assured. A cathedral was established in the Eastern settlement at Gardar (Igaliko), a monastery and a nunnery were founded, and twelve parish churches functioned in this settlement at the height of Greenland's prosperity. It has been calculated that at its greatest period some three thousand people lived in the two main settlements. The sad story of the rise, decline and eventual fall in the late fifteenth century of medieval Greenland cannot be told here as most of the story lies outside the period covered by this book. At the end of the Viking Period Greenland was an established area of settlement looking for the expansion of its economy to the unknown and as yet unexplored districts of the North (a runic inscription of 1333 at Kingigtorssuaq, between latitude 72° and 73°N, records how three Norse-Greenlanders had wintered there). Excavations in Greenland by Danish archaeologists have revealed much of this later medieval settlement in some detail, but little has been revealed of the Viking Period proper, save for some buildings at Brattahlid, of which only one is documented – the eleventh-century church of Thjodhild. This had curved walls of turf and was very small – about 2 m × 3·75 m.

The discovery of America

Bjarni Herjolfsson discovered America by accident about 985. Bjarni had returned home from Norway to Iceland to find that his parents had left to settle with Erik the Red. He decided to join them with his companions and set out. 'Our voyage', he said, 'will seem foolhardy, since not one of us has ever sailed into the Greenland Sea.'

> Nevertheless they set out immediately they were ready and sailed three days before losing sight of land. Then their following wind failed, and north winds and fogs overtook them, so that they did not know where they were going. This continued over many days . . . before sighting land. They wondered among

76

themselves what land this could be. Bjarni said that he thought it could not be Greenland . . . 'I think we should sail close into the land.' This they did, and could soon see that this was not a mountainous land, but wooded and with low hills . . . Bjarni's men asked him if this was Greenland; he said that he did not think so . . . 'for there are said to be huge glaciers in Greenland'.

Bjarni never actually landed in America but turned back to Greenland, and it was left to Leif, son of Erik the Red, to land in North America and give names to it: *Helluland*, *Markland* and *Vinland*. The story of these and subsequent voyages are told in the sagas of the Greenlanders and of Erik the Red and in one or two other less coherent sources.

While there can be no doubt that the Vikings discovered America or indeed that some Vikings spent some time there – it is recorded, for example, that Thorvald, Leif's brother, lived there for two years until he was killed by the local inhabitants – and may have meant to settle in the country, opinions differ widely concerning alleged Viking antiquities discovered on the North American continent. Much of this evidence can be dismissed as of no account; the Newport tower in Rhode Island has been thought to be a Viking structure, but in form it is exactly paralleled by a seventeenth-century English windmill; the runic stone from Kensington in north Minnesota was almost certainly faked by a local farmer of Swedish descent, and is certainly not genuine; the find of Norwegian weapons from a site at Beardmore, near Lake Nipigon, in Ontario, in 1930 was almost certainly salted, though it is just possible that it is genuine. Other minor evidence must be dismissed; but a site excavated by the Norwegian author, Helge Ingstad, and his archaeologist wife at L'Anse aux Meadows in northern Newfoundland has at last produced a site dated, by the radiocarbon method, to the Viking Age. Two finds of objects from the site – a spindle-whorl, for weighting the spindle for spinning wool, and a ring-headed pin – are the only movable objects of Viking Age date found on the site. The house types are related to those in the Scandinavian settlements. This site must be considered as a semi-permanent settlement of a group of Vikings who probably lived in this area in the eleventh century. They can certainly not be identified with any known historical character and least of all with Leif Erikson, who wintered one year at a place he named *Leifsbuðir*.

In recent years the dramatic find of the alleged fifteenth-century Vinland Map and the great publicity given to its discovery has focused attention once again on the Norse discovery of America. The ballyhoo surrounding this extraordinary document – which is now clearly demonstrated to be a fake – has led to frequent reports of new Norse sites on the North American continent, the most recent of which is a report from Laval University of a 'twelfth-century settlement' and 'navigational beacons' seventy miles up the coast from Payne Bay in the Ungava Peninsula. It must be emphasized that only informed excavation by skilled excavators with experience of Viking Age sites can possibly substantiate surface observations by untrained archaeologists. Such statements are worth following up, but should in no way be accepted at their finder's immediate interpretation.

That the Vikings discovered America is accepted by all but a few scholars who insist that Irish priests got there before them. Nothing should detract from the Viking achievement in this direction, and yet neither the Vikings nor the rest of the known world were able to utilize this discovery. The lines of communication were too long, there was richer economic potential nearer at hand in Iceland and Greenland, they adventured only along the coast – perhaps as far south as New England – and up one or two rivers, into a few inlets, and could not use the potential which they saw there. They had neither the wealth, the people, nor the organization to develop these new lands and, while the achievements of Bjarni and Leif were never quite forgotten in northern Europe, they achieved a legendary-like quality which was not known to the merchant venturers of Genoa and the Mediterranean in the late fifteenth century. In 1347 (less than 150 years before the voyage of Columbus!) Icelandic annals record the last remarkable event concerning Markland, and thereafter Scandinavian contacts with America are unrecorded.

Ships and navigation The Viking achievement in the West was only accomplished as a result of fine seamanship and skilful shipbuilding. The great ships preserved in Oslo and Roskilde are among the most impressive remains of the Viking Age: no one can stand unmoved in the Viking Ship Museum in Oslo, for the skill of the shipwrights eleven hundred years ago produced in the Gokstad ship an object of admiration for all sea-going people.

It has been suggested above that the sail was perhaps introduced into northern waters before the Viking Period, but in the ninth century we have positive proof of the sailing-ship in the great vessels found in the graves of southern Norway, Tune, Oseberg and Gokstad. The Gokstad ship is the most impressive of these vessels, at once a symbol of wealth and power and of the potentiality of the Viking in the western seas. An exact copy of the Gokstad ship sailed in 1893 to the U.S.A., as a pointed reminder to the Americans (who were celebrating Columbus's fourth centenary) of previous visits to their shores, and the experienced master, Captain Magnus Andersen, who commanded this copy could not praise her too highly:

> . . . we often had the pleasure of darting through the water at speeds of 10, and sometimes even 11, knots. This in spite of a primitive and relatively small rigging! Whether the old Norsemen used their ships in the same way as this is hard to say, but it does not seem unlikely that they used the ships for all they were worth. It seems absolutely certain that in those days too they wished to travel as fast as possible; why else should they have taken the trouble to improve the structure until it was so perfect that not even the shipbuilders of our time can do better as far as the ship's bottom is concerned. The fact is that the finest merchant-ships of our day, those regarded as the best sailers, have practically the same type of bottom as the Viking ships.

Many types of vessels were used by the Scandinavians in the Viking Period. The rowing-boat (*bátr*) was usually distinguished by the number of oars, a *feræringr* for example had four. The chief vessel for coastal and shallow waters was the *karfi* and this was sometimes used as a warship. The true warship, however, was the long ship (*langskip*), but it may have been difficult in many ways to distinguish this from the *hafskip*, or sea-going vessel, which is sometimes known as a merchant vessel (*kaupskip*). Ships could be used for many purposes and it is difficult to give the Gokstad ship a specific label; *langskip* would cover the weapons found in it, though its sea-going qualities would justify labelling it as a *hafskip*, but perhaps it would be better described as a general-duties vessel.

Section through the Gokstad ship, showing the clinkered construction. The upright T-shaped feature amidships is one of a pair of crutches which would carry spars and possibly even the mast, when it was unstepped. In this position the spars would form a ridge for a tent, which would be erected when the ship was hove-to at night. The immense size of the mast-fish at deck level and of the mast-seating on the keel give some indication of how sturdy and workman-like this vessel was.

The Gokstad ship is the best documented of the Viking ships, and a description of it will serve as a guide to the type of vessel used in the Viking Age. Slight typological advances can be seen as the Viking Age progresses and ships of later date, like those raised from the bed of Roskilde fjord (used to block one of the approaches to the town of Roskilde in the early eleventh century), the Swedish finds from Galtabäck and Falsterbo (dated by radiocarbon analysis to the late eleventh and early twelfth centuries), enable us to follow certain changes of the design throughout this period. At each end of the scale, ships like those from Kvalsund, discussed above, and thirteenth-century vessels or fragments from Asker and Bergen in Norway enable us to view the whole sequence of northern shipbuilding.

The Gokstad ship is built of oak – only the decking, mast, yards and oars are of pine. It is 23·3 m overall and 5·25 m amidships. With a load of 8 tons it would draw approximately 74 cm, a draught which might increase to 92 cm when fully loaded. The keel, which is made of a single T-shaped piece of timber, is joined to members at each end which rise to form prow and stern-post which possibly terminated in a curving tip. It is clinker-built, the planks overlapping each other and being lashed to the rather slight ribs of the vessel by pliable roots of spruce. Cross-beams above the water-line, supported on inverted L-shaped pieces of timber, tied the whole vessel together. The third plank below the gunwale was pierced by oar-holes which were closed when the vessel was under way. The planks were nailed together by iron rivets clenched over washers. The mast was seated in a housing of great blocks of wood attached to the keel; it was probably about 10 m long and could easily be raised or lowered. The sail was carried on a single yard, 11 m long, and was of white wool with sewn-on red stripes. The oars were probably only used in inland water for manoeuvring in harbour or in adverse weather conditions. It was steered by a large oar attached to the starboard (literally: steering side) side of the stern. With the vessel were found a large number of pieces of shipboard equipment – anchor, gangplank, spars and bailers.

This was a light vessel, and the method of attachment of the planks to the ribs gave her an elasticity which enabled her to rise to the waves without the structure being too badly shaken.

As time went on the form of the Viking ships developed, but in general terms did not differ greatly from that of the Gokstad vessel. The stepping of the mast, for example, seems to have become more efficient in the course of the Viking Age; the keelson becoming longer, until, in the Middle Ages, its length approached that of the keel itself.

Preliminary reconstructions of two block ships sunk in the eleventh century, found at Skuldelev, near Roskilde, Denmark. Each vessel had a well for cargo amidships and oar-holes only at prow and stern, where the vessels were decked. Note the tiller of the lateral steering oar at the stern.

The navigational practices of the Viking Age have been much discussed. To a large extent their ships were sailed within sight of land, but when ships crossed the seas to the Western Isles, to Iceland or to America, some form of navigational aid must have been used. Presumably the stars and the sun were used in such a context, and there is some evidence that bearing dials and azimuth tables were used as further aids. The Vikings seem to have had a fair idea of latitude, but none of longitude; they probably used a method of reckoning, known from later periods, by means of which they would sail to the latitude of their destination and then follow this parallel until land was sighted. On well-known passages, like that to the Faroes, they were probably able to sail by an almost direct route.

Detail of the ornament on a memorial stone from Alskog, Gotland, Sweden, portraying a wagon. On the only surviving Viking example, the funerary cart from Oseberg (see pl. 17), the axle-trees are connected by a beam, and it also had spoked wheels and a pair of shafts connected by a chain.

Land transport

We are so fascinated by the ships of the Vikings that it is easy to forget that they also travelled great distances by land. The trade route from Uppland in Sweden to Tröndelag in Norway, for instance, was not negotiated by ships but by horses, sledges and even carts, while the great ox-road south from the north of Jutland into Germany was used widely, presumably by quite sophisticated forms of transport. In winter, passage over snow and ice was fast , and the presence of large numbers of skates in the archaeological levels at the Swedish town of Birka indicated the importance of travel on ice, as does the presence of iron spikes which could be attached to a horse's hooves so that they would not slip on the frozen lake.

The horse was important. Bridles, spurs, saddles and (for the first time) stirrups are found in archaeological contexts, while horseshoes are mentioned in Icelandic texts. For the horse as a pack animal we must rely on the literary evidence. One such source, *Grettirs Saga*, tells of a man buying 'much fish and carrying it away on seven horses.' The horse was used as a draught animal as can be seen from pictorial representations on tapestry and stones. Horse-collars are found in Denmark, but whether oxen or horses were used to pull the ceremonial wooden wagon found in the Oseberg ship-burial, or the carts which made the ruts on the road revealed in the Lindholm excavations, is not known.

Bone skate (left) from a grave at Birka, shown from the side and the top, made from the metacarpal of a horse. The Norse word for a skate means 'ice-leg-bone'. Horses were shod with iron spikes (above) in winter to facilitate riding on snow or ice. These examples were found at the feet of a horse in a grave at Birka, an island which can be approached over the ice during the winter.

From the same Norwegian grave at Oseberg, which provided us with a wagon, come a series of sledges which have bodies attached to the runners by means of struts. Earlier, at the beginning of our era, dug-out sledges are known; these were presumably used for transporting goods on snow or grass. Similar sledges undoubtedly continued in use for a considerable period; their function was probably entirely different from that of the frame sledges found at Oseberg, which would be used almost exclusively on snow. But for simple transport on snow, skis and skates were used. Skates, indeed, were already being used in sporting contexts, and as a test of general manly prowess: in the *Heimskringla*, for example, one man says to another, 'I was so skilful on skates that no one could beat me, and you could no more do it than an ox.'

Winter travel necessitated the use not only of skates and skis, and spikes for horses, but of sleds, like this 'simple' sledge from the Viking ship-burial at Oseberg, Norway. To the basic wooden frame would be fastened a plain, box-like body, and the whole would be pulled by a pair of horses.

Trade and towns   The westward adventures of the Vikings were largely caused by a search for wealth, either in the form of goods or land. The distinction between the pirate and the merchant is a fine one and it is to the latter activity that we must now turn our attention, for the mechanics of trade were responsible for the eastern expansion which some would see as resulting in the foundation of the Russian state and which brought to Scandinavia wealth and to spare from the Arab and Byzantine worlds. As we have seen, throughout the first millennium the population of Scandinavia had traded over long distances; in the Roman Iron Age vast quantities of luxury items were brought into the North, while for much of the succeeding four hundred years trade, even if it fluctuated, was always there, bringing wealth from the South and East to the men of the North. During the Viking Period this trade grew and prospered, and the establishment of towns and major market-places is symptomatic of this activity. Helgö in the heart of the rich kingdom of Uppland was succeeded by the greatest of all the Viking market-places, Birka, a trading station with all the attributes of a town, as we can learn from the Western European sources which describe journeys to this teeming metropolis by the first missionaries to the North. The site of Birka is well known from both literary and archaeological sources. It is on an island in the great Mälar lake, which pushes into the heart of Uppland from the Baltic Sea, and lies on the route from the royal centre of Uppsala to the outside world. Within a semicircular bank, probably originally capped by wooden battlements, is a 29-acre site in the centre of which, by the water's edge, is an area of settlement, known as 'the Black Earth' because of the colour of its soil. The whole site is dominated by a fort which is built outside the line of the wall. Only a small area of this enclosure has been investigated archaeologically; we know very little of its appearance, of the shape of its houses, of its street system; all we have is evidence of industry – bone, pottery, metalworking, jewellery. Excavations are planned which should uncover more of the town, whose importance is indicated by the 1,200 graves outside the walls. These graves, excavated in the last century, show that the town flourished from about 800 to 950/975, and that it had commercial connections with all the known world, particularly with the East. Coins, pottery, metalwork, skins, silks, glass and other objects found here, demonstrate a lively contact with Britain, with the Carolingian and Byzantine empires, with the caliphates of western Asia, with Russia, with the Lapps and with the other Scandinavian kingdoms. Inside the walls of this town the merchants would meet to bargain: Frisians, Swedes, Britons, Germans, perhaps even Arabs, would gather to trade under the protection of the King's representative and buy the goods produced by the local inhabitants – antler combs, jewellery, leather goods, as well as food and drink. They would come by sea, tying up their ship in one of the harbours outside the town or drawing it up on the shallow beach inside the walls, which was protected by a palisade of stakes set in the water: in the winter traders would come by skis, skates and sledge over the frozen lake. For nearly two centuries this was the most northerly major mercantile centre of Europe.

There were, however, other towns – other markets. Some were small, perhaps even seasonal camps, dealing with local trade or with merchants seeking a specific type of goods. In certain parts of Norway, for instance, there was a specialized industry which produced soapstone bowls and other vessels, which were apparently in great demand throughout Scandinavia and would be sold at the markets. Other towns within the Viking sphere of influence were large and flourishing – bigger even than Birka. Such a town was Hedeby on the neck of the Jutland Peninsula; planted on the edge of the Schlei fjord it had easy and protected access to the sea. Excavations within the great bank of this town have revealed mercantile contacts similar to those found at Birka. This was a town mentioned by two travellers at the English court of Alfred the Great – an Anglo-Saxon, Wulfstan, and a Norwegian, Ohthere – they called it *Hæðum* and they had both traded there. Another place mentioned by Ohthere was *Sciringesheal*, in the south of Norway, five days' sailing from Hedeby. *Sciringesheal* has been identified by Norwegian historians and archaeologists as Kaupang (*lit.* 'market') in Tjölling, Vestfold. Kaupang is now set on a shallow bay, between rocky hills; in the Viking Age, when the sea-level was 1·8 m higher, it was a natural harbour protected by a string of islands and shoals. Since, moreover, the market-place had a natural defence of hills, there was no need for the bank encountered at Birka and Hedeby. Excavation here has again produced many imported goods, although objects of Eastern origin are comparatively rare. Kaupang was obviously not so rich as the other two towns, but it must have been one of the main outlets of trade for Vestfold, one of the richest areas in Norway.

83

Other towns are known to have been founded in Scandinavia in the course of the Viking Age, but not all have been investigated thoroughly; Västergarn on Gotland, for example, Other towns, such as Sigtuna and Lund, seem to have developed later; these functioned not only as local market-places but also as cult places, administrative centres and, with the coming of Christianity, as episcopal sees. The Vikings also founded towns and trading stations in the colonies. Dublin was founded by the Vikings in the 830s; originally it was a fortified base, later it became an extremely important port, its international character being hinted at in Arabic, Norse, English and Irish sources. Excavations in Dublin have uncovered important industrial areas of the Viking town, one of the cemeteries of which (at Islandbridge, Kilmainham) has been known for many years. The Vikings founded other towns in Ireland, but in England and elsewhere they took over existing towns. Some, like Dorestad in Holland, were already considerable trading centres, others, like York, were given a more mercantile character than they had hitherto had.

In Eastern Europe the pre-Viking Scandinavians already had considerable economic interests on the south coast of the Baltic. One of their sites there – Grobin, near Liepaja (Libau) in western Latvia – was investigated by a Swedish archaeologist between the wars: it seems to have been a town of para-military character under the control of soldiers from central Sweden, but functioning, nevertheless, as a trading station. By the early years of the ninth century the Vikings were in control of a North Russian town, Staraja Ladoga. The complicated story of Swedish-Russian relations is discussed below; suffice it to say here that trade is practically the whole basis of the Viking activities in the East.

Internal trade also flourished. Into Scandinavia poured silver and gold, rare spices, silks and fine woollen cloth, wine and exotic bronzes; but the market which supplied the Frisian merchant with slaves, furs, ropes and honey also supplied the local farmer with his iron knife and the salt to preserve his meat. Internal trade could be on a fairly large scale, iron and soapstone, apparently transported over great distances, being two materials particularly in demand in the home market. To a certain extent this trade could not have existed without a standard of exchange; this was silver – either in the form of coin or as bullion. Although there was a reasonably satisfactory Scandinavian currency from time to time, there was no real monetary economy until the end of the Viking Period; the merchant relied on the weight of the silver he received, and among the commonest antiquities found in merchant graves – as in earlier periods – are small pairs of portable scales, which would be used in the market-place to check the silver in any transaction. Perhaps because there was no effective royal control of currency in the tenth and eleventh centuries, vast quantities of foreign coins circulated in Scandinavia. Viking Age hoards in Sweden have yielded 34,000 Anglo-Saxon coins, 80,000 Arabic coins and 154,776 Frankish or German coins. Although the Danish and Norwegian totals do not by any means measure up to these – there are only 3,300 Anglo-Saxon coins recorded from Norway and only 5,300 from Denmark – the importance of silver to the Scandinavians cannot be underestimated. The fact that silver was treated as bullion is emphasized by the fact that many of the hoards contain pieces of broken and cut silver (hack-silver), often bits of old or outmoded jewellery or plate, cut into pieces for the purpose of trade. It may be assumed the Vikings accepted a coin at its face value in its country of origin (where rigorous standards were imposed) and by weight at home, where the coins themselves were often cut to balance the scales.

84

It has been shown how, since the Roman Iron Age, the Scandinavians had been in intermittent contact with the eastern Mediterranean by way of the great rivers of Eastern Europe. Viking presence in Russia is denied by nobody, but for nearly two hundred years argument – based on nationalism – as to the importance of this presence has been raging fiercely. There are two schools of thought, that of the *Normanists* (mainly Scandinavians) and that of the *anti-Normanists* (mainly Russian): the Normanists believe that the Vikings founded the great towns of European Russia and hence laid the foundation of the Russian state; the anti-Normanists hold that the Russian state is of Slav origin. Although the anti-Normanists have been the most virulent, the Normanists have themselves quite often been unreasonable. While tending to an acceptance of the Normanist viewpoint, I am not swayed too greatly by some of their more resounding statements. The roots of the problem lie in the identity of a people called *Rus* who appear in the Russian Primary Chronicle (*Povest Vremennykh Let*). Between 860 and 862, according to the Chronicle, the inhabitants of central European Russia invited a number of men 'who were known as *Rus* just as some are known as Swedes, others Northmen, others Angles (*i.e.* from Angeln in South Jutland) and others Goths (*i.e.* from Gotland), to bring order to their country'. Three brothers came: Rurik, the eldest, settled in Novgorod, while the others (who died within a few years) settled in Beloozero and Izborsk. 'On account of these *Varangians* [Scandinavians] the district of Novgorod became known as the land of the Rus.' This is merely a summary of a complicated story told by a later chronicler who was more than a little muddled by geographical terms and historical events,

The Vikings in the Baltic and Russia. This map shows the rivers that formed their main trade routes.

indeed the word Varangian itself was not apparently used until the tenth century. The origin of the word *Rus* has not been satisfactorily explained, although it has been alternatively suggested that the word is derived from the Finnish *Ruotsi*, or from the Old Norse *ródr* (a rowing-way), or again that these men came from the Roslagen in Uppland, Sweden. The way they are described in the Russian Chronicle in the company of other Scandinavian people would imply their northern origins, while the lively tradition that they founded the great city states of Russia (particularly Novgorod and Kiev), which is strongly attested in other sources both eastern and western, is hard to gainsay. How long they retained their Scandinavian character is, however, quite another matter.

The Vikings came to Russia for purposes of trade, long before Rurik was invited to Novgorod, and they developed there two major routes, one along the Dnjeper and the other along the Volga. The former is described by the Russian Primary Chronicler: 'Starting from the Greeks, this route proceeds along the Dnjeper, above which a portage leads to the Lovat. By following the Lovat, the great lake Ilmen is reached. The river Volkhov which flows out of this lake enters the great lake Nevo [Ladoga], which opens into the Varangian [Baltic] Sea.' It was along this route that the great towns of Kiev, Smolensk (or its predecessor), Novgorod and Staraja Ladoga are situated, and it is along this route that quite a considerable body of Viking archaeological material has been assembled. The second route exploited by the Vikings was to the east, and here there was no possibility of settlement on the same scale, as large towns had long been established to control the fur trade; this control was exercised by the rulers of the Bulgars and Khazars in the region of the Volga, who charged a toll on traders. From the Bulgar bend it was possible for the traders to strike out across the desert to reach the silk route to Baghdad and China somewhere near the Aral Sea. Though the documentation is scanty, Arab sources and archaeological finds encourage the belief that it was of some importance, and it was probably along this route, rather than through Byzantium, that many of the Arabic coins found in Scandinavia had travelled. It was probably in this area that the Vikings came into contact with Arab writers such as Ibn Fadlán who give the first graphic descriptions of the *Rus* and of their strange customs. A third, but less dramatic, eastern trade route passed down the Oder and Neisse to link up with the great east-west trade route from Mainz to Kiev by way of Cracow, and to the Danube and the rich markets of south-central Europe and the Mediterranean.

Excavations at Novgorod, Staraja Ladoga and Kiev, as well as at Gnezdovo (the cemetery of the precursor of Smolensk), have produced some Scandinavian material, but not in sufficient quantities to enable us to form major judgments concerning the pattern or chronology of the Viking incursion. At Staraja Ladoga, the only town in which major ninth-century levels have been reached, the evidence is equivocal as the foundations of the buildings excavated seem to be of Finnish rather than Scandinavian character. At the Gnezdovo cemetery a fair amount of Scandinavian material has been recovered – although Russian archaeologists would say that the amount is minimal. At Novgorod only a small area of the original town has yet been excavated and only in one portion of this has any ninth-century material been recovered. Nevertheless Novgorod was thoroughly influenced by the Vikings. As late as the eleventh century a Swedish rune-master was inscribing the name Novgorod (Holmgarðr) on a memorial stone at Sjusta, Skokloster, Uppland, in an inscription in memory of four men, one of whom, Spjallbude, 'died in Holmagrðr

86

The medieval Russian city of Novgorod. Excavations (shown by the numbers) have unearthed finds that are completely Slav in character. The kremlin, or fortress, is in the centre of the west bank of the river.

in Olaf's church'. The fact that there was a church dedicated to the Scandinavian royal saint Olaf in Novgorod in the eleventh century speaks volumes for the Swedish presence there.

But, as in Normandy and in England, the Scandinavian settlers in Russia quickly adapted their lives to that of the Slav tribes among whom they were living; the fact that the houses discovered at Ladoga are built in a Finnish style is no more significant than the fact that when they came to England the Vikings erected crosses of an Anglo-Saxon form over the graves of their dead. The Vikings of Ladoga were traders not craftsmen: when they wished to build a house they employed local labour, and the local labour-force built in the native tradition. The foundation and control of Novgorod, Smolensk and Kiev were necessary to the security of one of the major routes to the East, and the importance of this to the Vikings is emphasized by the fact that most of the seven major rapids on the Dnjeper bear names of Scandinavian origin. As long as the rulers of the great towns maintained amicable relations with their Scandinavian cousins it would not matter how Slavicized they became. In a town largely peopled by slaves, artisans, craftsmen and merchants who would be Slav and where the only Scandinavians would be a few strong-arm characters among the riff-raff of the ruler's bodyguard, it would soon be inevitable that the leading men of Kiev and Novgorod would adopt the major elements of Slav civilization and the orthodox religion of the Byzantine Eastern Empire. However, even as late as the eleventh century, one of the greatest of the Kievan princes, Yaroslav, was conscious enough of his Scandinavian heritage to marry the daughter of Olaf Skötkonung, King of Sweden, and give hospitality to the exiled Harald Haraldsson (Harald Hardrada) of Norway, who later became King of Norway and was to suffer defeat and death at the hands of the Anglo-Saxon King Harold at Stamford Bridge in 1066.

Trade was not, however, the only reason for the Vikings' eastward journeys. At all times the Viking was a mercenary soldier of skill and loyalty who fought for reward wherever he could find employment. Having been brought up in a heroic tradition he was willing to fight and die for the man he chose as lord, whatever that man's nationality. On many of the Swedish rune-stones from the ninth century onwards there are references to men who died 'eastwards in Greece' (i.e. Byzantium) or in Russia. At Ed, near Stockholm, was found a long inscription:

> Ragnvald had the runes cut in memory of his mother Fastvi, Onäm's daughter. She died in Ed. God help her soul. Ragnvald had the runes cut, he was in Greece, he was the leader of the host.

This surely refers to the Norse mercenaries, the Varangian Guard, who served the Emperor in Constantinople (Miklagarðr): Ragnvald, a man of high birth, had reason to boast if he had commanded these crack troops. By the middle of the eleventh century the Varangian Guard had ceased to be a specifically Scandinavian institution; other foreigners, English and French, were converting it to a kind of foreign legion. As the Varangian Guard lost its Viking character, so the Scandinavian connections with the East gradually declined, only the rune-stones telling us of a continuous contact until at least 1060.

4 The Vikings at home

In considering the great adventures of the Vikings overseas it is easy to forget their presence in their homeland, where they enjoyed the fruits of their external contact, whether mercantile or piratical. In general it is true to say that the Scandinavians of the Viking Age were not fundamentally different from their ancestors who have been described earlier in this book. The Viking who had travelled outside his homeland was different only in outlook from the home-bound Scandinavian of the Migration or Vendel Period. The tenor of life at home was very much the same, the economy was basically agrarian, the sea and the lakes provided food, houses were built, cloth woven, children born; people prospered or failed to prosper, as did their forebears. There seems to have been no dramatic economic change in Scandinavian life inside the homeland around 800. For one reason or another the Viking adventure overseas began about then, but people's lives were little affected by these developments.

The social structure of Viking society conformed to a norm well known in contemporary Europe, a norm which can be explained with misleading simplicity. At the bottom of the social scale was the slave (*þræll*), a term which covered a wide class of men from a bankrupt to a captive in war; the son of a slave was also a slave. At home he was employed on the farm; he represented capital to his owner and could be sold abroad without difficulty in the markets of Europe and the East. The life of a slave was of no account, and it is by no means unknown to find a sacrificed slave in a Scandinavian grave – an excavation at Ballateare in the Isle of Man provided a clear example of this practice. The slave's life could be hard, but it paid a slave-owner to keep his possessions in good trim, and for many a Scandinavian who was a slave in his own land the life was not too animal. Gradually, through the influence of Christianity, many slaves were freed and their lot improved; eventually a slave could even earn his freedom by his own efforts.

The free peasant (*karl*) was by no means entirely free; if he had been a slave, or if his family was of slave stock, he still owed service to the family of his erstwhile master. In ideal circumstances he owned his own land, but in practice he more often hired his services to a master, or held land in exchange for service to the proprietor. His class provided craftsmen and soldiers: some were pedlars, some may even have been merchants. They had protection under the law and played some part in its administration. It was probably from this class that many of the bands of Viking marauders and traders were raised by the tough young aristocrats who financed the expeditions. The free-men who went on these expeditions would often have been the dissatisfied younger sons who saw no chance of bettering their position on the family's holding, and who had now a chance to win wealth and even land across the sea.

The third class consisted of the aristocrat (*jarl*) or chieftain. Basically he was a warrior who had gathered a warlike band around him and united his area of the country. In the course of the Viking Age this class of society began to hold land from the king in a proto-feudal manner. This process was to some extent responsible for the proper establishment of the Scandinavian kingdoms by depriving the *jarl* of his independence – an independence that had resulted in a lust for wealth which he had previously satisfied by acts of piracy or trade. The process of centralization was hastened by the influence of the Church, which needed the support of a strong centralized power, and by the growth of merchant guilds, which introduced certain restrictive practices that hurt the freebooter. The centralized kingdom grew, developing feudal ideas of military service; the king imposed taxes, established and added to his own estates and hence to his private wealth.

Throughout this period the Scandinavian depended on the land for his basic livelihood. Cattle, horses, sheep and goats were bred for milk and meat; crops were planted, grown, harvested and ground to make bread, porridge and beer; fruit was collected from the forests and heaths. Farming was becoming more intensive and breeding more selective; the Norwegian farmer, for example, developed to the full the practice of transferring cattle to high pasture-lands during the summer months, as is witnessed by the greater number of burials in these mountainous areas during the Viking Age. Sheep were of great importance in the Atlantic islands and Iceland, and being hardier could often survive the winter without the flock being thinned too much. Sheiling sites were probably developed at this period.

It is difficult to trace Viking settlement patterns in the countryside. Village sites are scarce, although many scholars are willing to explain this by the assumption that the villages of the Viking Age are covered by modern settlements. In many areas, notably Iceland, Greenland and some of the colonies, there is plenty of evidence for scattered single farms, and one has the suspicion that the nucleated settlement was a rarity in Scandinavia. In Denmark, however, a number of 'villages' have been excavated. Chief among them are Aggersborg (which was destroyed in the late tenth century to make way for a military fortification), Sædding and Lindholm Høje in North Jutland. Lindholm may not in many respects be typical, for it had a trading function and was the centre of a metalworking industry. It dates from the eleventh century and partly overlies an early Viking Age gravefield. At least four different types of house were recognized: small huts with sunken floors, large rectangular houses, at least one house with bowed sides and, strangest of all, a courtyard house. This latter, which was to become the standard form of Danish farm-house in this area, is at this period only paralleled at the great Danish fortified sites at Trelleborg, Fyrkat and Aggersborg. The single-farm complex is perhaps better documented in the archaeological record, mostly in Iceland and the Atlantic isles. At Jarlshof on the southern tip of the mainland of Shetland, for example, is a complex of buildings which excavation has shown to have been in continuous occupation by a Viking chieftain throughout the Viking Age. But the most dramatic remains were excavated at Þjórsárdalur in Iceland. An eruption of the volcano Hekla in 1104 devasted this valley and the fields and buildings of some twenty or more farms. Þjórsárdalur was first settled at the time of the colonization of Iceland at the close of the ninth century and the eruption buried the earliest period of this valley's history.

Soon after the establishment of the settlement it became clear to the colonists that the large rectangular house, which since the beginning of our era had been the main type of building in Scandinavia, was not suitable for the windswept island to which they had come. The great spaces were broken up and the various farm-buildings were clustered together into one irregular complex, the smithy and byre alone being built at some distance from the main farm. Large halls were not unknown in Iceland, a splendid example was revealed at the beginning of this century at Hofstaðir, but they are rare. The houses were built of turf laid on two courses of stone, the main room lined internally with wainscotting. At one of the most typical of these farms, that at Stöng in Þjórsárdalur, the main hall had benches along each long wall on either side of a central fire-place. The main bed was in the entrance hall in an alcove and various rooms – dairies, storage space, kitchen and guest-room – were added higgledy-piggledy to the house as the need and opportunity arose.

Within houses such as these a considerable farming community lived, the slaves sleeping in the hall or in the kitchen, and most of the main activities taking place in the same two places, which were always warm. At mealtimes the master of the house would sit in the 'high seat' placed at the centre of one side of the hall, and tables, perhaps in richer houses spread with a linen cloth, would be brought in. The high points of home life at this period were the feasts, which often lasted several days. The story-telling of a skilful entertainer together with the weak beer brewed by the ladies of the house, perhaps a little imported wine, special food, and then more beer would break the monotony and isolation of the long winters of the North. In pagan times the local religious festivals were accompanied by great feasts, and the coming of Christianity did not change the pattern. Other entertainments included board games and field sports of a semi-organized nature:

> . . . and people came from the west from Midfirth and from Waterness and Waterdale all the way, and from out of Longdale, and there was a great gathering together . . . Now the sports were set going and Hall took the lead. He asked Kjartan to join in the play. . . . The game went on all day long, but no man had either the strength or litheness of limb to cope with Kjartan. And in the evenings when the games were ended, Hall stood up and said, 'It is the wish and offer of my father that those men who have come so far should stay here over night and take up the games tomorrow' . . . there were over a hundred men in the house that night. And the next day sides were divided for games again.

The continuity of the civilization of the North throughout the first millennium is strongly emphasized by Viking art, for the decoration applied by the Scandinavians to their everyday objects follows closely in the tradition which first emerges at the end of the Roman Iron Age. This fact so struck the French historian Marc Bloch that he used it as an illustration of the self-confidence of the Vikings in that, although they came into contact with the more sophisticated art of the Carolingian and Ottonian empires, they never let this seriously affect their own individuality. In the Viking Period we see the existing animal art brought to new heights, and only with the introduction of plant ornament, towards the end of the tenth century, did their art begin to lose its vitality.

The early Viking Age provides us, by a fortunate chance, with an opportunity to witness the art of the North in its most natural medium – wood. The great ship recovered from the grave of a Viking queen or princess at Oseberg, in South Norway, is by no means as fine a sea-going vessel as that from Gokstad, but it is itself decorated with the finest ornament of Style III, and on other wooden objects in the grave are further expressions of this style which surpass anything seen in the preceding period. Two basic motifs are used in the ornament of these objects: the first is a beast with a small head, openwork panels in its hips and a frond-like extension to its limbs and to its pigtail; the second is a series of animals massed

Art

Animal art through the Viking Period. Top: detail of the ornament of a rectangular brooch from Skabersjö, Skåne, Sweden, showing the typical ribbon-like animal of Style D; it was this late Vendel style which heralded the early Viking styles, represented centre and far right. A detail of a carved animal-head post (centre) from the Oseberg ship-burial displays three gripping beasts; while a detail from the Oseberg stern post (far right) illustrates how the animals of Style E are interlaced. Their legs sometimes develop into tendrils which further help to bind the motif together. The animal ornament (bottom) drawn from a silver cup found in a royal grave at Jelling gives its name to the Jellinge style. Note the loop or lappet at the lip, the sinuous double-contoured body of the animal and the pigtail.

together so that the limbs constitute the most obtrusive feature, gripping the nearest element of the ornament with their paws. This motif is simplified in one of the two succeeding styles, the so-called Borre style – named after another rich burial. One of the main elements in this style is an animal with a head at the top of the field, the body forming a slow curve below the head to form a hip on either side. Other motifs include a specific ring-chain motif, which we encounter later in the Isle of Man, and a lion-like beast. The style emerges about the middle of the ninth century and traces linger until the end of the tenth century; it was universal in Scandinavia and particularly popular in Viking contexts in Russia.

More or less contemporary with the Borre style is the Jellinge style, which probably began towards the end of the ninth century and continued until about 1000 – dates based on coin hoards and on its occurrence in an early phase of the Viking settlement in England. It is named after the animal which decorates a small silver cup from the Jutland village of Jelling, the royal necropolis of Denmark: this animal has a ribbon-like body, a pigtail and a lip-lappet. Developing naturally out of this is the animal of the succeeding style – the Mammen style – which is a substantial creature with foliate offshoots of acanthus-leaf form, appearing at its most typical on bone and on stone. The Mammen style may be roughly dated to between 970 and 1010 and fines into the Ringerike style in which the acanthus leaf is elongated into great tendrils which often seem to take over the whole pattern – the Ringerike style is particularly popular in stone sculpture, and takes its name from a group of ornamented slabs in the rich district of Norway which bears that name. It was also for a short time popular in England where it blended with, and perhaps influenced, the later development of the elaborate and rather lush Winchester style during the reign of Cnut and the other Danish kings of the eleventh century. Ringerike ornament grew naturally in the mid-eleventh century into the last truly Viking style – the Urnes style – with its smooth, sinuous fighting animals, which appear in all their decadent perfection on the fascinating reconstructed stave church at Urnes in Norway.

This outline of a vital art is intended to explain the sequence of the styles seen in the accompanying illustrations. It is an art which may seem to be vulgar in the way that baroque art is vulgar. The Viking artist could not bear to see an empty space, every square centimetre had to be filled with contorted and coiled creatures. The roots of the art lay in the Germanic past of Scandinavia, and if it ever had any meaning, that meaning had by this time been lost. It had little restraint, and only on the runic memorial stones of Sweden and on one or two other objects decorated in the Urnes style does a certain cleanness of line give it a quality which is almost to the modern taste. Technically this ornament is a fantastic achievement; let us enjoy its technique even if we may not approve its form.

The coming of Christianity

Save in the island of Gotland (where there had been a continuous tradition since the end of the Roman Iron Age), decorative stone carving was unknown in Scandinavia until the middle of the tenth century, when, possibly under English influence, the custom of raising ornamented memorials in stone was initiated. One of the first such stones comes from the Danish royal cemetery at Jelling in Jutland. It is a semi-pyramidal boulder of red-veined granite, rather more than 2·5 m in height; one face bears a lion in the Mammen style caught up in the coils of a snake, the second face a primitive representation of the Crucifixion, while the third face carries an inscription:

> King Harald ordered this stone to be raised in memory of Gorm his father and Thyra his mother. [He was] that Harald who won all Denmark and Norway, and made all the Danes Christian.

The Harald referred to is Harald Bluetooth (940–85) and the stone was probably set up between 983 and 985.

The events which led to the conversion of Denmark in the middle of the tenth century had started much earlier. The first recorded attempt to convert the Danes had been made by the English missionary, Willibrord, in the early years of the eighth century. He met with no success, but brought back with him thirty Danish youths, perhaps with the intention of founding a seminary. Various attempts were made in the following years to convert the Danes, but they generally came to nothing. In the early thirties of the ninth century a German monk, Ansgar, at the behest of the Emperor Louis the Pious, journeyed to Birka in Sweden and converted a fair number of people, including the official representative of the King, a man called Herigar, who built a church on his estate. The missionaries returned to Germany after two years' work among the pagan Swedes. Ansgar, the apostle of Scandinavia, later became Bishop of Hamburg and, after the sack of this town by the Danes in 845, Bishop of Bremen in plurality with Hamburg; from there he founded a church in Schleswig in which many Danes were baptized. Meanwhile the missionaries he had sent to Birka

93

had been expelled – one, Nithard, had been killed – but about 850 Ansgar dispatched a priest to Birka and, some two years later, went there again himself. After a certain amount of initial obstruction he received the support of the King, who bought out of his own pocket a house for one of his missionaries, Erimbert. At all times the missionaries in the North appear to have been treated with tolerance, although there were often short periods of persecution during which a church or mission-station might be closed. The conversion of the North was slow, but was not carried out by force, rather by argument and conviction.

In 935 the break-through came for the Christian missionaries. One of Ansgar's successors as Archbishop of Hamburg and Bremen (Unni) went to Denmark and managed, through Harald Bluetooth the King's son, to get permission to preach throughout Denmark. He then went to Birka only to find that the Swedes had reverted to paganism. It was there that he died in 936. As early as 948 sees were established with German missionary bishops in Denmark at Hedeby, Ribe and Åarhus. Harald became Christian between 960 and 965, probably for political reasons, for at about the same time he submitted to the Emperor Otto I, whom he recognized as overlord.

It was probably about this time that Norway also became influenced by Christianity – Håkon the Good who died c. 960 was a Christian – but it is not until the reign of Olaf Tryggvason, who came to the throne in 995, that Norway officially adopted the new faith – at the point of the sword. This forcible conversion was not very effective, and it was during the reign of St Olaf (1014–30) that the Norwegians were finally converted by both English and German missionaries. Iceland was converted in 1000 by act of the Althing:

> Then it was made law that all people should be Christian and those be baptized who still were unbaptized in this land; but as to exposure of children the old law should stand and also as to eating of horseflesh. People might sacrifice to heathen gods secretly, if they wished, but under penalty of the lesser outlawry if this was proved by witnesses. But a few winters later this heathendom was abolished like the rest.

Sweden, however, was still basically a pagan country and despite the formal acceptance of Christianity by King Olaf Skötkonung in 1008 and his foundation of the bishopric of Skara, it was probably not until well on into the twelfth century that the Swedes became Christian and the great temple at Uppsala, described by Adam of Bremen, was destroyed.

Conclusion

Cast-bronze figure of the Norwegian saint and king, Olaf, on the Irish reliquary of St Manchan, probably made between 1120 and 1130.

The Church landed pen in hand, and as the North became part of the literate European Christian community its vitality was strangely sapped and the Viking Age came to an end. The tenth and eleventh centuries saw the Scandinavian countries at the peak of their international importance; never again were they to make the same impression on European life. Achievements of latter-day Scandinavian heroes of the stamp of Gustavus Adolphus and Charles XII pale into insignificance beside the conquests and explorations of the Vikings. The vital civilization which the classical authors at the beginning of the millennium had only dimly perceived in the Pythean mists had risen like a star to its zenith – an object of wonder and fear to the world of the succeeding millennium.

94

Select bibliography

This select list of books is intended partly as a guide to further reading and partly as a list of the more fundamental books concerned with the period covered by this book.

GENERAL (archaeology)

Brøndsted, J. Danmarks Oldtid, 2nd ed., vol. iii, København 1960

Klindt-Jensen, O., Denmark before the Vikings, London 1957

Hagen, A., Norway, London 1967

Kivikoski, E., Finland, London 1967

Shetelig, H., Falk, H. and Gordon, E. V., Scandinavian Archaeology, Oxford 1937

Stenberger, M., Sweden, London 1963

Wilson, D. M. (ed.), The Northern World, London 1980

GENERAL (history)

Steenstrup, J., Normannerne, København, 1976–82

Turville-Petre, E. O. G., The heroic age of Scandinavia, London 1951

THE ROMAN IRON AGE

Eggers, H. G. Der römische Import im freien Germanien (Atlas der Urgeschichte, I), Hamburg 1951

Stjernquist, B., Simris, on cultural connections in the Roman Iron Age, Lund 1955

Wheeler, R. E. M., Rome beyond the Imperial frontiers, London 1954

THE MIGRATION AND VENDEL PERIODS

Gjessing, G., Studier i norsk merovingertid, Oslo 1934

Klindt-Jensen, O., Bornholm i folkevandringstiden, København 1957

Sjøvold, T., The Iron Age Settlement of Arctic Norway, Tromsö/Oslo 1962

THE VIKING AGE (General)

Arbman, H., The Vikings, London 1961

Foote, P. G. and Wilson, D. M., The Viking Achievement, London 1970

Jones, G., A history of the Vikings, Oxford 1968

Kendrick, T. D., A history of the Vikings, London 1930

Sawyer, P., The age of the Vikings, London 1962

SETTLEMENT

Ambrosiani, B., Fornlämningar och bebyggelse, Stockholm 1964

Hagen, A., Studier i jernalderens gårdssamfunn, Oslo 1953

Hougen, B., Fra seter til gård, Oslo 1947

Petersen, J., Gamle gårdsanlegg i Rogaland, Oslo 1936

Stenberger, M. (ed.), Forntida gårdar i Island, København 1943

Stenberger, M. and Klindt-Jensen, O., Vallhagar, Stockholm 1955

ART

Almgren, B., Bronsnycklar och Djurornamentik, Uppsala 1955

Holmqvist, W., Germanic Art, Stockholm 1955

Salin, B., Die altgermanische Thierornamentik, Stockholm 1904

Wilson, D. M. and Klindt-Jensen, O., Viking Art, London 1966

PAGAN GODS AND RELIGION

Chadwick, H. M., The Cult of Othin, Cambridge 1899

Turville-Petre, E. O. G., Myth and Religion of the North, London, 1964

Olsen, O., 'Hørg, Hov og Kirke', Aarbøger for nordisk oldkyndighed og historie, 1965

SACRIFICAL OFFERINGS

Englehardt, C., Denmark in the Early Iron Age, London 1866

Hagberg, U. E., The archaeology of Skedemosse, Stockholm 1967

Stjernquist, B., 'Präliminarien zu einer Untersuchung von Opferfunden', Meddelanden från Lunds universitets historiska museum, 1962–3, 5–64

RUNES

Arntz, H., Handbuch der Runenkunde, Halle 1944

Jansson, S. B. F., The Runes of Sweden, Stockholm 1962

VIKING GRAVES

Arbman, H., Birka I, Stockholm 1940

Bersu, G. and Wilson, D. M., Three Viking graves in the Isle of Man, London 1966

Brøndsted, J., 'Danish inhumation graves of the Viking Age', Acta Archaeologica, VII (1936), 81–228

Ramskou, T., 'Viking Age Cremation Graves in Denmark', Acta Archaeologica, XXI (1950), 137–182

Strömberg, G., Utersuchungen zur jüngeren Eisenzeit in Schonen, Lund 1961

THE VIKINGS IN WESTERN EUROPE AND BRITAIN

Arbman, H. and Stenberger, M., Vikingar i Västerled, Stockholm 1935

Collingwood, W. G., Scandinavian Britain, London 1906

Loyn, H., The Vikings in Britain, London 1977

Shetelig, H., Viking Antiquities in Great Britain and Ireland, Oslo 1940–54

THE VIKINGS IN THE EAST

Arbman, H., Svear i österviking, Stockholm 1955

Arne, T. J., La suède et l'orient, Uppsala 1914

Blöndal, S., The Varangians of Byzantium, Cambridge 1978

Grekov, B. G., Kiev Rus, Moscow 1959

Stender-Petersen, A., Varangica, Århus 1953

Vernadsky, G., The origins of Russia, Oxford 1959

THE VIKINGS IN THE NORTH ATLANTIC

Eldjárn, K., Kuml og Haugfé úr heiðnum sið í Íslandi, Akureyri 1956

Ingstad, A. S., The Discovery of a Norse Settlement in America, Oslo 1977

Jones, G., The Norse Atlantic Saga, Oxford 1964

Krogh, K. J., Viking Greenland, Copenhagen 1967

Magnusson, M. and Pálsson, H., The Vinland Sagas, Harmondsworth 1965

SHIPS

Brøgger, A. W. and Shetelig, H., The Viking Ships, their ancestry and evolution, Oslo 1951

Brøgger, A. W., et al., Osebergfunnet, Kristiania

Nicolaysen, N., Langskibet fra Gokstad ved Sandefjord, Kristiania 1882

Olsen, O. and Crumlin-Pedersen, O., 'The Skuldelev Ships', Acta Archaeologica XXXVIII (1967), 73–174

Select bibliography (continued)

TOWNS AND TRADING STATIONS
Arbman, H., *Birka, Sveriges äldsta handelstad*, Stockholm 1939

Holmqvist, W. et al., *Excavations at Helgö*, Stockholm 1961 (in progress)

Jankuhn, H., *Haithabu, ein Handelsplatz der Wikingerzeit*, Neumünster 1956

COINS AND HOARDS OF THE VIKING PERIOD
Grieg, S., 'Vikingetidens skattefund', *Universitetets Oldsaksamlings Skrifter*, ii (1929), 177–312

Malmer, B., *Nordiska mynt för år 1000*, Lund 1966

Skovmand, R., 'De danske Skattefund fra Vikingetiden', *Aarbøger for nordisk oldkyndighed og historie*, 1942, 1–275

Stenberger, M., *Die Schatzfunde Gotlands der Wikingerzeit*, Stockholm 1947–58

DAILY LIFE
Hald, M., *Jernalderens Dragt*, København 1962

Petersen, J., *Vikingetidens Redskaper*, Oslo 1951

LITERATURE AND CHRONICLES
General surveys of Icelandic literature in English will be found in S. Einarsson, *A history of Icelandic literature* (New York 1957), and G. Turville-Petre, *Origins of Icelandic Literature* (Oxford 1953). Many sagas have been translated into English, and the reader is referred to editions published by Penguin, Oxford University Press, Messrs Nelson and Messrs Dent (in the Everyman series).

Sources of illustrations

MUSEUMS AND COLLECTIONS

Aarhus, Museum: sword, photo: Holger Arbman (81)

Bergen, Historisk Museum, University of Bergen: carved animal head (9)

Copenhagen, Nationalmuseet: painted glass cups (2); Roman jug (3); the Mammen axe (22); female skeleton (26); pottery (27); *terra sigillata* bowl (30); Roman vessels (31); swords (39); brooches (62); harness mounts, photos: Holger Arbman (68, 69); twelve axes (73)

London, Dept. of the Environment: reconstruction drawn by Alan Sorrell, Crown Copyright (71)
–British Museum: painting by W. G. Collingwood, photo: John J. O. Webb (87)

Man, Isle of, Manx Museum: churchyard, Balladoole (49); woman's skull, Ballateare (59); mound during excavation, Ballateare (60)

Oslo, Universitetets Oldsaksamling: decorated sword hilt (1); prow of Oseberg ship (7); carved tiller, photo: P. G. Maurtvedt (8); Gokstad ship (10); Oseberg head-post (11); carved head (12); carved head detail (13); iron rattle (14); shoes, photo: Mittet foto (15); kitchen equipment, photo: Mittet foto (16); Oseberg cart (17); chest (18); Hon hoard (21); gilt bronze weather vane, photo: P. G. Maurtvedt (23); stave church (25); square-headed brooch (37); sundry pieces from the Oseberg ship (50); excavation of the Oseberg ship (51); reconstructed Oseberg ship, Viking Ship Museum, photo: Mittet foto (52); Gokstad ship (53, 54); excavation of the Gokstad ship (55); oar hole with cover (56); decorated rowlock (57); small boats from Gokstad ship-burial, photo: Terje Olsen (58); corner post from sledge, Viking Ship Museum (67); detail from Oseberg cart (80)

Schleswig-Holstein Landesmuseum: reconstructed interior (33); man's shirt and stocking-breeches (41); aerial view of Hedeby (86)

Scotland, National Museum: Skaill hoard (20)

Stockholm, Statens Historiska Museum: Latin inscription from bronze vessel (4, 28); helmet from grave XIV, photo: ATA (5); helmet from grave I, photo: ATA (6); hoard from Birka (19); bridle mount (24); gold hoard from Timboholm, photo: ATA (35); bracteates, photo: ATA (38); household utensils, photo: ATA (42); loom weight, photo: ATA (43); drinking horn, photo: ATA (44); picture stone, photo: ATA (45); silver arm-ring (61); figures, photo: ATA (63); horse and rider, photo: ATA (64); Eketorp hoard pendant, photo: University Museum (65); silver pendant, photo: Holger Arbman (66); bronze Buddah, photo: ATA (74); hoard, Asarve, photo: ATA (75); game (76); bronze figure, photo: ATA (77); Thor's hammer amulet, photo: ATA (78); silver-gilt pendant cross, photo: ATA (79); head of a warrior, photo: ATA (82)

PHOTOGRAPHERS AND ARTISTS

Anderson, Iwar: silver brooches (32). *Antikvarisk Topografiska Arkivet* (ATA), Stockholm: house, Vallhager (36); the Årby boat, photo: G. Arvidsson (48); Ismantorp (83); runic inscriptions, Ed (89, 90); rune-stone, Skokloster (91). *Gadefors*, George: Hoard, Havor (34). *Gyldendal*, Copenhagen: Trelleborg, model (85). *Middlemas*, T.: Gosforth cross (93). *Olsen and Crumlin-Pedersen*: drawings on p. 80. *Rodd*, Lucinda: map on p. 72 (after the author), plans on pp. 85, 87. *Stenberger*, Prof. M.: Eketorp, photo: Rune Hedgren (84); rune-stone, Täby, Uppland (92). *Strömberg*, Dr M.: arm-ring, Vittskövle (29); neck-rings, Trolleberg, Flackarp and Ryd, Skabersjö (40); stone ship-setting, Vätteryd (46). *Wilson*, Eva: runic alphabet (88); line drawings on pp. 12, 16, 70, 71, 79, 81, 82, 92, 94